Illustrator:
Ken Tunell

Editor:
Charles Payne, M.A., M.F.A.

Editor in Chief:
Sharon Coan, M.S. Ed.

Art Director:
Elayne Roberts

Art Coordination Assistant:
Cheri Macoubrie Wilson

Cover Artist:
Tina DeLeon Macabitas

Product Manager:
Phil Garcia

Imaging:
Charles Payne, M.A., M.F.A.

Trademarks:
Trademarked names and graphics appear throughout this book. Instead of listing every firm and entity which owns the trademarks or inserting a trademark symbol with each mention of a trademarked name, the publisher avers that it is using the names and graphics only for editorial purposes and to the benefit of the trademarked owner with no intentions of infringing upon that trademark.

Publishers:
Rachelle Cracchiolo, M.S. Ed.
Mary Dupuy Smith, M.S. Ed.

INTEGRATING TECHNOLOGY into the Science Curriculum

CHALLENGING

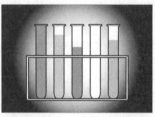

Author:

Debi Hooper

Teacher Created Materials, Inc.
6421 Industry Way
Westminster, CA 92683
ISBN-1-57690-429-6

©1999 Teacher Created Materials, Inc.

Made in U.S.A.

TABLE OF CONTENTS

TABLE OF CONTENTS *(cont.)*

INTRODUCTION

When I began my new job as a computer resource teacher several years ago, I scanned all the popular teacher book catalogs for something, for anything, that would give me some ideas of how to help teachers integrate the use of computer technology and, later, the World Wide Web into their curriculum areas. I found plenty of materials about how to use various software packages but not about how to effectively blend them with regular lessons. Hopefully this book, and this series, will help technology coordinators, resource teachers, media specialists, and classroom teachers find ways of incorporating the use of computers and other peripheral devices into the curriculum they already know and love.

Part one of *Integrating Technology into the Science Curriculum* will focus on some computer basics as well as the management involved in using the various technologies available in your school. There will also be a section to guide you through successful searching on the World Wide Web.

The second part of *Integrating Technology into the Science Curriculum* provides you with lesson plans which will correlate with science concepts taught in grades 5–8. Keep in mind as you read these that they are not "etched in stone." Once you read one lesson idea, it may spark several others.

There will be several URL (Universal Resource Locator) addresses for World Wide Web sites included with each lesson. These are not all the possible sites, but they will provide you with a starting point to help you find additional background information, lesson ideas, or sites where you can download free or inexpensive software. As is the nature of the ever-changing Web, some addresses may change over time. Hopefully, there are enough listed with each lesson that you will have the opportunity to connect to several. To visit a Web site for which a URL is listed, simply key that address into the "Location:" space of your browser and press Enter.

There is also a section devoted to sharing some great ideas sent in from other teachers. Although they are not complete lesson plans, they will provide you with a glimpse of how more teachers are using technology in their classrooms.

Integrating Technology into the Science Curriculum is an excellent resource book for science and computer teachers who are looking for ways to incorporate technology into their lessons and to lead students toward effective use of the World Wide Web.

YOUR COMPUTER

COMPUTER SYSTEM FUNCTIONS

- Input—data is entered into the computer from a keyboard, mouse, scanner, etc.
- Processing—the central processing unit of the computer uses the input to perform a function based on the software program you are using.
- Output—the result of processing is produced as either a view on your monitor or a "hard copy" on paper from your printer.
- Storage—information is stored on floppy or hard diskettes for later use.

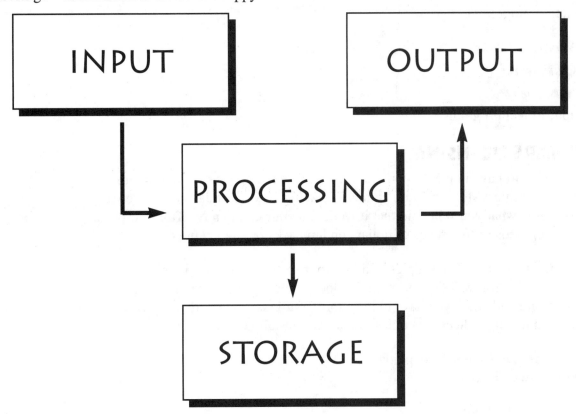

HARDWARE

- CPU—central processing unit
- Monitor
- Keyboard
- Mouse
- Disk Drive(s)
- Printer
- Other peripheral devices:
    modem
    speakers
    microphone
    CD-ROM drive
    scanner
    digital camera(s)—still images or video

YOUR COMPUTER *(cont.)*

BASIC TYPES OF SOFTWARE

System software:

DOS—disk operating system—this software gives instructions to your basic hardware components so that they will work together.

Applications software:

This is software that completes a certain task (such as word processor, database, spreadsheet, or presentation programs).

- *Microsoft Works*
- *ClarisWorks*
- *Netscape*
- educational programs

SOFTWARE LICENSING

A good policy to have in place about buying software for your lab or classroom is to always preview prior to purchasing. Most software companies will give you 30 days to preview a software package to make sure it is what you want and that it works on your computers. This is especially important before investing hundreds or thousands of dollars on lab packs or site licenses.

Another good idea is to keep copies of all of your software licenses in a binder in either your classroom or computer lab. You will then have all the documentation organized if you need to justify ownership of the software and when you have to inventory your classroom. Always keep in mind that we teach by example and having unlicensed copies of software installed on our computers is illegal.

Software Publishers Association
http://www.spa.org/

Copyright Web Site
http://www.benedict.com/

U.S. Copyright Office Home Page
http://lcWeb.loc.gov/copyright/

SOFTWARE LICENSING (CONT.)

Freeware/Public Domain/Postcardware:

This is free software which has been made available for you to use. Some programs may be student projects they are willing to share. In the case of postcardware, the programmer simply wants you to send in a postcard telling him or her where you are and how you are using the program.

> Freeware Central
> http://www.ptf.com/free/

Shareware:

This software is available for you to preview for free, usually for a 30-day trial period. Then you are asked to register it with the programmer. It is not substandard software—shareware is simply a different marketing strategy: a try-before-you-buy offer.

> Association of Shareware Professionals—This organization was formed to strengthen the future of shareware (user supported software) as an alternative to commercial software.
> http://www.asp-shareware.org/

> Shareware.com
> http://www.bsoftware.com/share.htm

> Jumbo Shareware
> http://www.jumbo.com/

> Shareware Shop
> http://www.bsoftware.com/share.htm

Commercial Software:

These programs are advertised and sold in catalogs and stores. In the case of educational software, you should be able to have a preview period, but the vendors are not required to allow that.

> Educational Software Cooperative—ESC is a non-profit corporation bringing together developers, publishers, distributors, and users of educational software.
> http://www.edu-soft.org/

TELECOMMUNICATIONS

WHAT DO I NEED?

In most cases, for you and your students to get online, you will need four pieces of equipment:

1. **Computer**

   Almost any current PC or Macintosh will allow you to get online, although there are still Commodore and Apple users accessing bulletin board systems and e-mail.

2. **Modem**

   Your modem is the peripheral device that allows your computer to communicate with other computers via a telephone line. Current modem speeds are 28.8 bps and 33.6 bps and higher, but you will still be able to access many services with a 14.4 bps modem.

3. **Phone Line**

   A basic phone line dedicated to only computer use is preferable. The line should have touch-tone dialing rather than rotary and should not have a call-waiting feature added. (You will not need a modem or phone line if your school has a direct connection to the Internet via fiber optic cabling.)

4. **Telecommunications Software**

   This software is provided by your Internet service provider (ISP) and is pre-configured to dial in to their server. You can also use the telecommunication utility in such software packages as *Microsoft Works* to dial in to some host computers and bulletin board services.

TELECOMMUNICATIONS (cont.)

I'M ONLINE—WHAT DO I DO NOW?

Once you get online, there are many programs which will allow you to connect to different services or sources of information via the Internet. Most of those services will be accessible through your World Wide Web browser, a program designed to connect you with various resources online.

E-mail, or electronic mail, is a means of sending written messages over a telecommunications connection. You can also attach other files, such as graphics and sound files, spreadsheet, or database files, to the e-mail in order to transfer them from your computer to the recipient's computer. E-mail is a simple but powerful way to share information and collected data in a timely manner.

Mail lists, or list servers, are automated bulk mailing organizations. There are many educational list servers that you can join. E-mail is sent in from one participant on the list and is automatically forwarded to all members to read and respond to.

The World Wide Web (or Web) and Internet browsers, such as *Netscape Navigator*, *Microsoft Internet Explorer*, or *Mosaic*, make accessing information much more user-friendly than other individual software programs. These browser programs allow you to see pictures, hear sounds, view animations or movies as well as find text information from a variety of sources.

You should discuss the reliability of resources with your students prior to their doing research online. Anyone can post information on the Web. Students need to learn how to differentiate between authentic information and those Web pages that are simply interesting but not factual.

Throughout this book, there will be URL (Universal Resource Locator) addresses given for a variety of sites on the World Wide Web. You can access those sites by keying in the address in the location blank of your browser and pressing enter. That should take you on a journey to a Web site with information about that topic. But, what happens if you want more information or information about a different topic? In order to find more information, you would use a search engine, an online database of Web sites with a search capability.

Excite
http://www.excite.com/

AltaVista
http://altavista.digital.com/

Infoseek
http://www.infoseek.com/Home?pg

Ultraseek
http =ultra_home.html

Yahoo!
http://www.yahoo.com/

Web Search Strategies–Finding Something That's Relevant
http://www.mispress.com/Websearch/Websch4.html

TELECOMMUNICATIONS *(cont.)*

HOW DO I KEEP STUDENTS FROM FINDING THINGS THEY SHOULDN'T SEE?

Prior to allowing students access to the Internet from any site in your school, you should have an acceptable use policy (AUP) in place. This should be a part of your technology plan and should include student instruction about the policy once it's in place. Parental support of the use of the Internet within your school is important. A presentation at a teacher-parent organization meeting might help parents see the value of having the Internet as a resource in today's world of education.

Sample Acceptable Use Policies
http://www.usoe.k12.ut.us/curr/Internet/aup/aupdir.html

WLMA ONLINE : Acceptable Use Policies
http://www.wlma.org/libint/aups.htm

Global School Network—Guidelines for Developing AUPs
http://www.gsn.org/Web/tutorial/issues/aupguide.htm

Your second line of defense might be a filtering software program. There are quite a few on the market. Basically, they block access to sites which are part of their database of undesirable sites. Be advised that they do not block access to all undesirable Web sites. New sites are being added to the Web daily, and you will need to make arrangements for continual upgrades of these software programs.

Cyber Patrol
http://www.microsys.com/cyber/

Surf Watch
http://www.surfwatch.com/

Net Nanny
http://www.netnanny.com/netnanny/

Cybersitter
http://www.solidoak.com/cysitter.htm

MANAGEMENT

This book will give you some lesson plans that you can tailor to fit your technology resources, but where do you begin doing just that?

TIME MANAGEMENT

Time management will be of major importance and will depend primarily on how many computers you can access at one time. If you only have one computer in your classroom, then you might need to divide your class into teams and have them rotate through the computer activity while you have the other students working on another part of the lesson. If you have a computer lab in your school, then you will need to make sure to schedule your time in the lab as soon as you know you need it so that your lesson will run smoothly and efficiently.

If you need to divide your class into teams, think about how to best accomplish the goal of the activity. For the most part, heterogenous grouping will be your best solution. Students at different learning ability levels will see things from different perspectives as they work on the computer and will make different contributions to the project. If you choose to use the technology activities as extension activities for your gifted students, then homogenous grouping for the entire lesson might be a better strategy.

Computer lab use will ensure that all students have access to the computer. This would be better for those activities requiring the use of databases or those in which students should make spreadsheets or corresponding graphs. You should also make sure to schedule weekly visits to the computer lab if you plan to have students use the computers while creating their science projects. Always remember that the lab is your school's way of equalizing the differences between those students who have access to computers at home and those who do not.

BEHAVIOR MANAGEMENT

Behavior management should follow the same rules as your regular classroom rules or those rules set in place by the computer lab manager. You should also address ethical computer use and safe use of electronic and computer equipment. Make sure your students understand basic rules about copyrights and plagiarism. These rules still apply when dealing with electronic media just as they do when dealing with printed materials. They should also be instructed in how to use all peripheral equipment prior to being left on their own to tackle it on a trial-and-error basis. Most pieces of equipment are very easy to use with proper instruction and very easy to break without instruction. In these cases, a little time invested in prevention is worth much time (and possibly money) in cure. Make simple reminder posters and post them near the computers or in a prominent place in the lab so that students won't have to continually ask questions about the use of equipment or software.

Most importantly—have fun using technology. If you become comfortable with it, then both you and your students will enjoy the activity more and the learning activity will be enjoyable.

MAJOR DIVISIONS OF SCIENCE

Students can research the divisions of science and present their information to the class.

Duration:

- 1 class period for research
- 1 or 2 class periods (per student or group) for creating presentations
- 1 class period for sharing presentations with the class

Materials:

- work sheet of divisions of science study
    - biology—the study of living things
    - oceanography—the study of oceans and the seashore
    - geology—the study of Earth, its composition and properties
    - meteorology—the study of weather, climate, and atmosphere
    - physics—the study of how matter and energy are related
    - chemistry—the study of matter and energy
- multimedia planning sheet (if students will be creating multimedia presentations)
- reference materials for research (science books, encyclopedias, electronic encyclopedias, online access)
- presentation software (*The Print Shop*, *HyperStudio*, etc.)

Before the computer:

- Allow students time to research the divisions.

On the computer:

- Students will create signs or multimedia stacks to explain their divisions and illustrate examples.

Option:

- Students could be grouped in teams of six with each student being responsible for one division, or the classroom could be divided into six teams with each team being responsible for one division. This will depend on how many computers you have available for students to use to create presentations.

Web Links:

Mr. Wizard's Home Page
http://www.mrwizard.org/

NYE Labs—Bill Nye, the Science Guy
http://nyelabs.kcts.org/

You Can with Beakman and Jax
http://www.nbn.com:80/youcan/

Name: _____ Date: _____

MAJOR DIVISIONS OF SCIENCE

BIOLOGY

CHEMISTRY		OCEANOGRAPHY

SCIENCE

PHYSICS		GEOLOGY

METEOROLOGY

1. Pick one division of science and use all available reference materials to find out what it is and to find some examples of what that type of scientist might be studying.

2. Using available software, create a brief presentation of the information you found.

Note:

You may use the back of this work sheet to take notes.

MULTIMEDIA PLANNING SHEET

Title Card

Buttons/Links: _____

Notes (Text/Sounds/Animations): _____

Card 1

Buttons/Links: _____

Notes (Text/Sounds/Animations): _____

Card 2

Buttons/Links: _____

Notes (Text/Sounds/Animations): _____

Card 3

Buttons/Links: _____

Notes (Text/Sounds/Animations): _____

Card 4

Buttons/Links: _____

Notes (Text/Sounds/Animations): _____

Card 5

Buttons/Links: _____

Notes (Text/Sounds/Animations): _____

SCIENTIST SEARCH

Students will research information about a scientist and then prepare part of a whole-class multimedia presentation.

Duration:

- 1 or 2 class periods for research
- 1 or 2 class periods for creating their part of the presentation
- Allow time for someone (teacher or student) to merge all the individual parts.

Materials:

- scientist search cards
- reference materials
- multimedia planning sheet
- sign-making/presentation/multimedia software (*The Print Shop*, *HyperStudio*, *Netscape Navigator*, etc.)

Before the computer:

- Copy the scientist search cards (laminate for future use) and cut them apart.
- Have students pick scientist cards from a hat or container.
- Allow students time to research the scientists.

On the computer:

- Students will each create a sign or multimedia stack to tell about their scientist and about his/her contribution to science and technology.

Sample HyperStudio Card

SCIENTIST SEARCH *(cont.)*

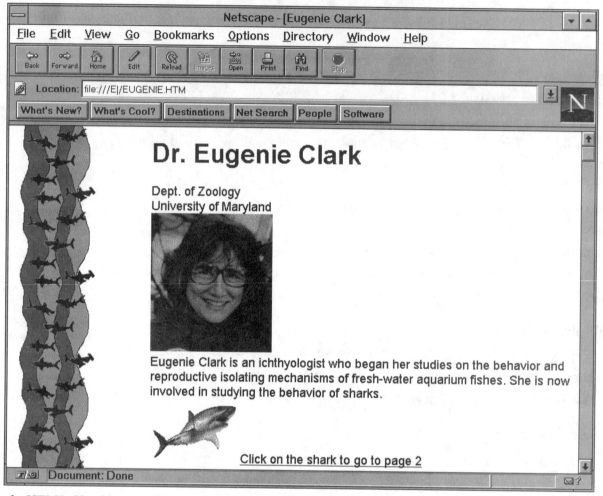

*Sample HTML file shown in **Netscape Navigator***

Options:

- You can use this activity with any list of scientists: biologists, women, ethnic groups, astronomers, etc.

List of additional scientists' last names:

Agassiz	Agricola	Alvarez	Ampere	Archimedes	Aristotle
Arrhenius	Audubon	Avery	Avicenna	Avogadro	Bacon, F.
Bacon, R.	Banting	Beadle	Beaumont	Becquerel	Bernard
Berzelius	Bohr	Boltzmann	Boyle	Brahe	Calvin
Carothers	Carver	Cavendish	Celsius	Chadwick	Chargaff
Clausius	Copernicus	Crick	Curie, M.	Curie, P.	Cuvier
da Vinci	Dalton	Darwin	DeVries	Ehrlich	Einstein
Faraday	Fermi	Fischer	Fleming	Franklin	Galen
Gallilei	Gauss	Gibbs	Goddard	Goeppert	Gray

SCIENTIST SEARCH *(cont.)*

List of additional scientists' last names: *(cont.)*

Grew	Hales	Halley	Harvey	Heisenberg	Helmholz
Herschel	Hershey	Hippocrates	Holmes	Hooke	Humboldt
Hutton	Huygens	Hypatia	Jenner	Jerne	Joliet
Joule	Kelvin	Kepler	Kirchoff	Koch	Krebs
Lamarck	Landsteiner	Laplace	Lavoisier	Lawrence	Leeuwenhoek
Linnaeus	Lister	Lyell	Maxwell	McClintock	Medawar
Mendel	Mendeleev	Meyerhoff	Miller	Millikin	Morgan
Muller	Newton	Nirenberg	Oppenheimer	Pasteur	Pauli
Pauling	Pavlov	Planck	Priestly	Ptolemy	Reed
Roentgen	Rutherford	Sabin	Sagan	Salk	Schrodinger
Seaborg	Teller	Thomson	Urey	Versalius	Watson
Wohler	Woodward	Wu	Young		

Web Links:

HSTM—Biographical Dictionary
History of Science, Technology and Medicine
http://www.asap.unimelb.edu.au/hstm/hstm_bio.htm

4000 Years of Women in Science
http://www.astr.ua.edu/4000WS/4000WS.html

The Faces of Science: African Americans in the Sciences
http://www.lib.lsu.edu/lib/chem/display/faces.html

Biographical Dictionary of Biologists
http://www.cshl.org/comfort/scientists/

Evolutionary Scientists
http://bubba.ucc.okstate.edu/artsci/zoo_home/zoo_lrc/1114www/evolutio/evolsci.htm

Biology Biographies
http://www.gene.com/ae/AE/SH/NSTA_NOR/doerder_biobiog.html

Shark clip art

Fiona's Shark Mania
http://www.oceanstar.com/shark

Shark Clipart
http://www.postmodern.com/~fi/sharkpics/clipart/clip.htm

SCIENTIST SEARCH (cont.)

THOMAS ALVA EDISON	NIKOLA TESLA
BENJAMIN FRANKLIN	JOHANNES KEPLER
SIR ISAAC NEWTON	CHARLES DARWIN
ALBERT EINSTEIN	MICHAEL FARADAY

SCIENTIST SEARCH *(cont.)*

GALILEO GALILEI	ANTOINE LAVOISER
JAMES CLARK MAXWELL	LOUIS PASTEUR
ERSNT RUTHERFORD	NICOLAUS COPERNICUS
EDWARD JENNER	JOHANN GREGOR MENDEL

SCIENTIST SEARCH *(cont.)*

MARIE CURIE	FRANCIS CLARK
JAMES D. WATSON	ENRICO FERMI
JANE GOODALL	WILHEM CONRAD ROENTGEN
CARL LINNAEUS	CHARLES BABBAGE

SCIENTIST SEARCH *(cont.)*

HANS GEIGER	**ROBERT HOOKE**
ERNEST LAWRENCE	**ALFRED NOBEL**
ROBERT J. OPPENHEIMER	**MAX PLANCK**
ALEXANDER GRAHAM BELL	**NIELS BOHR**

SCIENTIST SEARCH *(cont.)*

RACHEL CARSON	GEORGE WASHINGTON CARVER
GEORGE EASTMAN	AUGUSTE JEAN FRESNEL
EDMUND HALLEY	GRACE HOPPER
EDWIN HUBBLE	LINUS PAULING

SCIENTIST SEARCH *(cont.)*

DIANE FOSSEY	MARY LEAKEY
MARGARET MEAD	JACQUES COUSTEAU
EUGENIE CLARK	

MULTIMEDIA PLANNING SHEET

Title Card

Buttons/Links: _____

Notes (Text/Sounds/Animations): _____

Card 1

Buttons/Links: _____

Notes (Text/Sounds/Animations): _____

Card 2

Buttons/Links: _____

Notes (Text/Sounds/Animations): _____

Card 3

Buttons/Links: _____

Notes (Text/Sounds/Animations): _____

Card 4

Buttons/Links: _____

Notes (Text/Sounds/Animations): _____

Card 5

Buttons/Links: _____

Notes (Text/Sounds/Animations): _____

CLASSIFICATION OF LIVING THINGS

The structure of taxonomy will be reinforced as students continue adding organisms to a database of living things.

Duration:

- This could be an ongoing year-round activity.

Materials:

- reference materials
- database software (*AppleWorks*, *ClarisWorks*, *Microsoft Works*, etc.)
- database template file with the following fields:

  Common Name

  Kingdom

  Phylum

  Class

  Order

  Family

  Genus

  Species

Before the computer:

- The teacher (or student) should prepare the database template and insert several data entries (see example below).

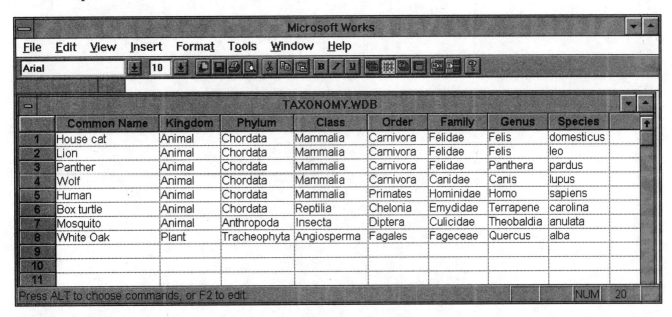

	Common Name	Kingdom	Phylum	Class	Order	Family	Genus	Species
1	House cat	Animal	Chordata	Mammalia	Carnivora	Felidae	Felis	domesticus
2	Lion	Animal	Chordata	Mammalia	Carnivora	Felidae	Felis	leo
3	Panther	Animal	Chordata	Mammalia	Carnivora	Felidae	Panthera	pardus
4	Wolf	Animal	Chordata	Mammalia	Carnivora	Canidae	Canis	lupus
5	Human	Animal	Chordata	Mammalia	Primates	Hominidae	Homo	sapiens
6	Box turtle	Animal	Chordata	Reptilia	Chelonia	Emydidae	Terrapene	carolina
7	Mosquito	Animal	Anthropoda	Insecta	Diptera	Culicidae	Theobaldia	anulata
8	White Oak	Plant	Tracheophyta	Angiosperma	Fagales	Fageceae	Quercus	alba
9								
10								
11								

On the computer:

- Students will key in new data entries and save the edited file.

CLASSIFICATION OF LIVING THINGS *(cont.)*

Options:

- This can also be used to organize information about organisms found in your town or a nearby river or lake or on a class field trip to a museum, zoo, or aquarium. You can then use this database for searching and sorting activities to analyze the bio-diversity in your area.

Web Links:

Taxonomy
http://bubba.ucc.okstate.edu/artsci/zoo_home/zoo_lrc/1114www/taxonomy/taxonomy.htm

Carolus Linnaeus
http://www.ucmp.berkeley.edu/history/linnaeus.html

Animal Bytes (by Busch Gardens—gives nomenclature for a variety of animals)
http://www.bev.net/education/SeaWorld/animal_bytes/animal_bytes.html

Classification (a sample unit plan)
http://curie.uncg.edu/~sbranz/classification.html

The Schools of Taxonomy
http://www.crl.com/~sarima/dinosaurs/philosophy/

CELL STRUCTURE

Students will learn the parts of plant and animal cells and will create presentations showing the similarities and differences.

Duration:

- 4–5 class periods (depending on computer access)

Materials:

- diagrams of plant and animal cells
- software program such as *Label That Diagram—Cells*
- presentation software (*Windows Paint*, *PaintShop Pro*, *HyperStudio*, etc.)
- multimedia planning sheets

Before the computer:

- Teach students the basic parts of the cells using charts and diagrams.
- Have students find descriptions of the functions of the various parts. ✔
- Students will plan their presentations on planning sheets.

On the computer:

- Students will create signs, diagrams, and multimedia presentations to illustrate the various parts of the cells—with descriptions of the parts.

Option:

- You could use this same format for students to illustrate and explain the parts of various things: parts of a flower, types of leaves, simple machines, electric circuits, etc.

Web Links:

Digital Graphics—various educational software available
http://members.aol.com/RTCCPU/Digital.htm

Label That Diagram—Cells—$15.00 Windows version
Cells: The Inside Story (a student project online)
http://www.nsysu.edu.tw/kas/home/classes/middle/proj/sci_cellproject/cells.htm ✔

Science Alive
http://www.sfu.ca/~yescamps/

Science Alive—Cell Cookie (online lesson plan)
http://www.sfu.ca/science-alive/1996_project_book/cell-cookie.html ✔

Virtual Cell—exploration of electron micrographs of a plant cell ✔
http://ampere.scale.uiuc.edu/~m-lexa/cell/cell.html

CELL STRUCTURE *(cont.)*

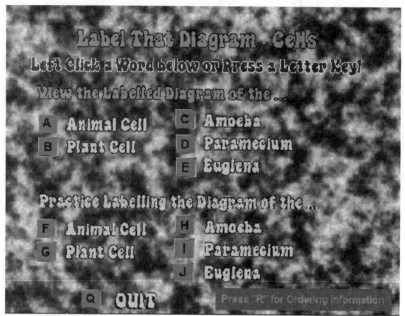

*Index Screen from **Label That Diagram—Cells***

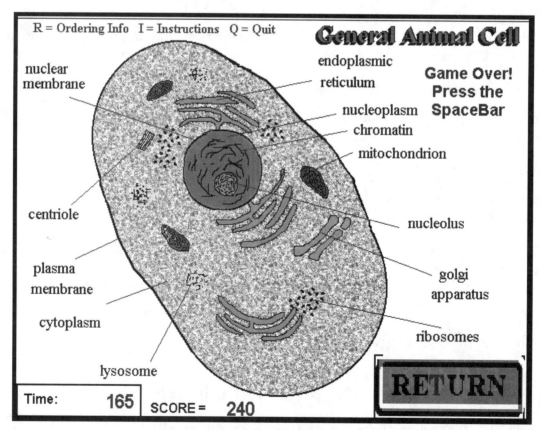

Students may study the labeled diagrams of animal and plant cells as well as amoeba, paramecium, and euglena. While playing the game, the labels appear and students must click in the right location for the label to move and for them to gain points.

CELL STRUCTURE *(cont.)*

ANIMAL AND PLANT CELL STUDY SHEETS

Animal Cell

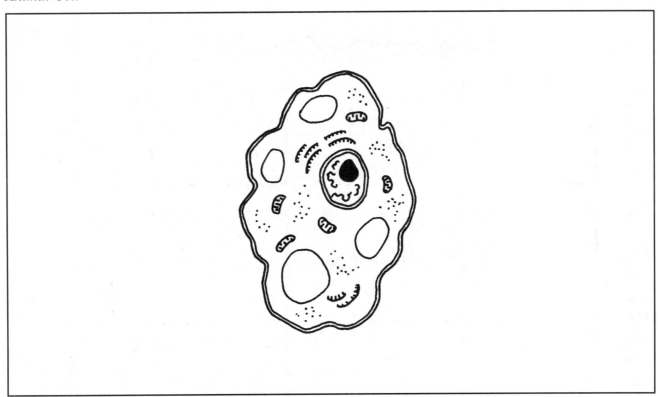

Plant Cell

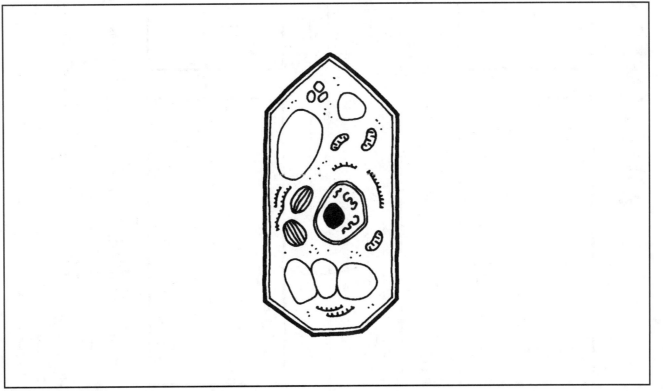

MULTIMEDIA PLANNING SHEET

Title Card

Buttons/Links: _____

Notes (Text/Sounds/Animations): _____

Card 1

Buttons/Links: _____

Notes (Text/Sounds/Animations): _____

Card 2

Buttons/Links: _____

Notes (Text/Sounds/Animations): _____

Card 3

Buttons/Links: _____

Notes (Text/Sounds/Animations): _____

Card 4

Buttons/Links: _____

Notes (Text/Sounds/Animations): _____

Card 5

Buttons/Links: _____

Notes (Text/Sounds/Animations): _____

DON T CUT THAT FROG!

Do you wish you could do that frog anatomy lesson without the cost and the mess and save some frogs' lives in the process? You can—with software and online access.

Duration:

- 2 to 3 class periods

Materials:

- software programs such as *Operation: Frog*, *Visifrog*, or *Frog Dissection*
- online access
- diagrams of frog anatomy

Before the computer:

- Assess students' knowledge base by having them draw pictures and label what they think they'll find inside a frog's body.

On the computer:

- Using either software programs or online access to one of the virtual frog dissection sites, have the students work through the steps of dissecting a frog.
- Have them label the diagram as they find the body parts.

Option:

- This could be a team project as other teams rotate through related tasks such as identifying local frogs or a study of your pond or stream environment. Students can create multimedia presentations about the anatomy of the frog or about the life cycle of amphibians (see The Frog Page Web site) or a photo presentation of the dissection (see Live on the Net).

Web Links:

Frog Dissection Sites

> NetFrog
> http://curry.edschool.virginia.edu/go/frog/
>
> The Whole Frog Project
> http://george.lbl.gov/ITG.hm.pg.docs/Whole.Frog/Whole.Frog.html
>
> Virtual Frog Dissection
> http://george.lbl.gov/ITG.hm.pg.docs/dissect/info.html
>
> Frog Anatomy & Physiology (photos with interactive labels)
> http://biog-101-104.bio.cornell.edu/BioG101_104/tutorials/frog.html

DON T CUT THAT FROG! *(cont.)*

cont.)

Frog Information Sites

Frogs and Other Amphibians
http://fovea.retina.net/~gecko/herps/frogs/index.html

The Froggy Page—links, graphics, etc.
http://frog.simplenet.com/froggy/

The Frog Page (created by a 14-year-old)
http://www.geocities.com/TheTropics/1337/index.html

Live on the Net—Frog Dissection
http://www.baxter508.k12.ks.us/liveonthenet/frog/frog.html

The Virtual Vivarium
http://www.esd113.wednet.edu/frogs/

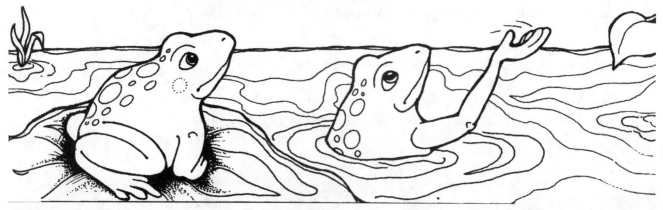

Name: _____   Date: _____

DON T CUT THAT FROG! *(cont.)*

Use the computer resources to help you label this diagram of a frog.

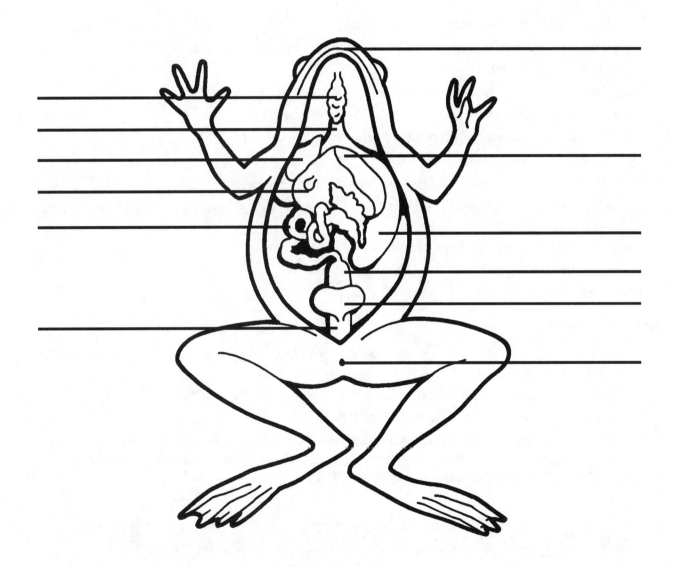

DIG FOR DINOSAUR DATA

With the recent rise in interest in dinosaurs, this activity is sure to be a crowd pleaser. Students, and you, can take this as far as you want it to go. It starts with a database and ends with a student-chosen project. Let their imaginations show with their own work.

Duration:

- 1 to 2 weeks, according to access to reference materials and depth of project ideas

Materials:

- reference works about dinosaurs (books, videotapes, software, online access)
- suggested software:

    Dinosaur Museum—Smithsonian Institution

    Dinosaur Discovery—AOMC or *150 Prehistoric Creatures*—ROMtech

    Dinosaur Encyclopaedia—HyperWorks

    Dinosaurs! The Multimedia Encyclopedia—Media Design Interactive

    Dinosaurs—Microsoft

    3D Dinosaur Adventure—Knowledge Adventure

    DinoPark Tycoon—MECC

- project backboards or cardboard (if you want to supply these for the students)
- desktop publishing software (*The Print Shop Deluxe*, *Serif PagePlus*, banner-making and sign-making programs)
- simple drawing program (*Paint*, *MacDraw*, *PaintShop Pro*)
- word processing, spreadsheet, and database software
- database about dinosaurs

Before the computer:

- Create a dinosaur database from guidebook data (ex: *The Dinosaur Encyclopedia* by Dr. Michael Benton, Simon & Schuster, Inc., 1984).
- Introduce the dinosaur concept with videos that explain living habits, etc.
- Assign students to teams or have them pick teams or partners.
- Establish a grading rubric that includes group cooperation, being on task, using multiple software products, following directions for the query, etc. (Students will respond better once they know what they will be held accountable for—everything!)

	Name	Pronunciation	Meaning	Order	Family	Period	Length (ft)	MLength (m)	Location
1	Acanthopholis	a-KAN-tho-FOLE-is	Prickly scales	Ornithischia	Ankylosauria	Cretaceous	18	5.5	England
2									
3									
4									

Data2

Sample database record—try to have at least 100 dinosaurs for variety.

DIG FOR DINOSAUR DATA *(cont.)*

On the computer:

- Use the database to have students practice searching, or querying, for multiple criteria.
- Have them follow the instructions for choosing a group of dinosaurs and creating a zoo or museum for them.
- They will need to rotate through the software reference materials, so have plenty of other resources available, as well (even if you have to borrow books from an elementary school for awhile).
- Have them use as many different software programs as you have available, for example:

  a database for querying for their group of dinosaurs

  a word processing program for writing small reports about one of their dinosaurs

  a spreadsheet for calculating the cost of admission or snack bar revenue

  a desktop publishing or banner/sign-making software for signs or labels for their displays

  a simple drawing program for creating maps of their zoos/museums

  a CD-ROM reference software for them to find information about their dinosaurs.

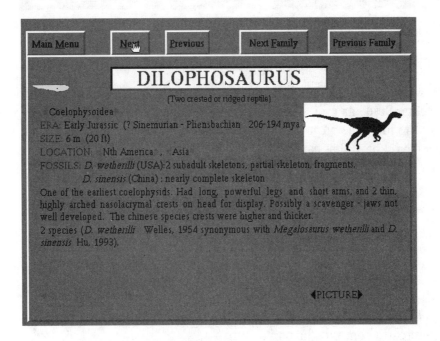

Screen shot from **Dinosaur Encyclopaedia** *by HyperWorks*

DIG FOR DINOSAUR DATA *(cont.)*

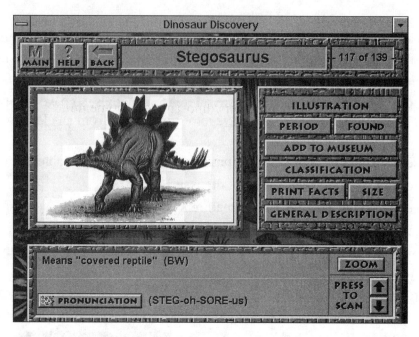

Screen print from **Dinosaur Discovery** *by AOMC*

Option:

- This activity works well as a culmination project after learning about word processing, databases, and spreadsheets. Students really show that the computer software technology is simply a tool to help them get the job done. You could also extend this project to include multimedia presentations if you have that capability.

Web Links:

Dinosauria Online
http://www.dinosauria.com/

Dinosaurs at the Smithsonian
http://photo2.si.edu/dino/dino.html

Scholastic's *The Magic School Bus—Age of Dinosaurs*
http://www.microsoft.com/kids/msbdinos.htm

Dorling Kindersley—Dinosaur Hunter Online
http://www.dkonline.com/preview/cdpreview/index.html

The Royal Tyrrell Museum
http://tyrrell.magtech.ab.ca/

The Dinosauria
http://www.ucmp.berkeley.edu/diapsids/dinosaur.html

DIG FOR DINOSAUR DATA *(cont.)*

Web Links: *(cont.)*

Texas Dinosaurs
http://www.tpwd.state.tx.us/adv/kidspage/dinos/txdinos.htm

Southwest Educational Development Laboratory—Dinosaurs
http://diogenes.sedl.org/scimath/pasopartners/dinosaurs/dinohome.html

Fossil Types—Dinosaurs
http://www.zoomschool.com/subjects/dinosaurs/dinofossils/Fossiltypes.html

HyperWorks Reference Software—Dinosaur Encyclopaedia
25 Clifton St., Scarborough, Western Australia, 6019 Dinosaur Discovery/150 Prehistoric
Creatures
http://www.romt.com/

Note:

Copy the following information for each team of students, particularly those designing zoos for their
"live" dinosaurs.

DATA FOR ZOOKEEPERS!

Make sure you don't put "meat eaters" in the same fencing areas with other dinosaurs, especially your
plant eating dinosaurs!   You know what might happen!

Herbivores (Plant Eaters)

Prosauropoda
Ornithopoda
Sauropoda
Stegosauria
Ankylosauria
Ceratopsia

Carnivores (Meat Eaters)

Coelurosauria
Deinonychosauria
Segnosauria
Carnosauria

Omnivores (Plant and Meat Eaters)

Ornithomimosauria

DIG FOR DINOSAUR DATA

TEAM INSTRUCTIONS

1. Each team will create either a dinosaur zoo or museum exhibit.

2. Each project will contain at least 15 dinosaurs.

3. Dinosaurs will be grouped according to at least one of the following:

   time period

   size

   location

   food eaten

4. The team will print a copy of the database query.

5. Using the word processing software, the team will prepare a set of instructions for someone else to follow to get the same query results.

6. Each person in the team will also prepare a short report about one of the dinosaurs in the team's project.

7. Each team will create a zoo map or museum exhibit diagram.

   It must explain why dinosaurs are grouped the way they are.

   Dinosaurs within the zoo or museum must be labeled so visitors will know what they are viewing.

   It should include other things found in zoos or museums (entrance, walkways, restrooms, gift shop, etc.)

8. Each team will create advertising for its exhibit. Signs must include

   type of display (zoo/museum),

   admission price(s), and

   information about specific dinosaurs.

9. Each team will create a display of the project (printed materials on backboards or cardboard, shadow boxes, multimedia presentations, etc.).

ANALYZING OWL PELLETS

Students are intrigued by the contents of owl pellets, once they start dissecting. This can lead to a database of the contents and a telecommunication project about owls with students in other regions of the country or other countries.

Duration:

- 1 or 2 class periods for dissecting the owl pellets and identifying and mounting the prey
- additional time on the computer to enter data about pellet contents

Materials:

- owl pellets or other raptor pellets (from a science supplier, raptor center, zoo, or "in the wild")
- dissecting tools (probes, pins, tweezers)
- magnifying glasses
- balance scale for measuring the mass of the pellet
- plain white paper (or thick paper plates) for dissecting trays
- zipper-top plastic bags for storage of bones, etc.
- cardboard (or thick paper plates) for mounting specimens after completely cleaning them (for classroom display)
- heavy-duty (clear drying) glue for mounting skeleton pieces
- chart or books with diagrams of skulls or skeletons of small prey
- database software

Before the computer:

- Depending on your resources, give an owl pellet to each student or pair of students.
- Have students observe the exterior of an owl pellet and then carefully dissect it, discarding any fur and feathers from the pellet and collecting and storing any bones for later identification.
- Using charts and books, have students identify the bones found in their pellets (skulls will be easiest to identify).
- They can record their findings on the lab activity sheet.
- Students will then mount the skeleton pieces on cardboard and label them appropriately for display in the classroom.
- Create a database template for students' data entries (add field for name of owl if you know more than one owl's pellets will be dissected).

On the computer:

- Students will enter data about their owl pellets into the class database.

ANALYZING OWL PELLETS *(cont.)*

PELLETS.WDB								
	Length	Width	Mass	Total # Prey	# Birds	# Rodents	# Insects	# Other	Names of prey
1									
2									
3									
4									
5									
6									

Sample database for recording owl pellet data

Options:

- Students near wooded areas or farms may be able to collect pellets "in the wild." These need to be dried before handling. (Do not store in plastic bags before drying thoroughly.) These owls or other raptors should be identified for comparison of pellet contents.

- A student in Minnesota used pellets collected and recorded by staff members at The Raptor Center and compared the digestion of prey by owls and hawks. His results can be found online at The Raptor Center's Web page.

- Data could be collected by students at more than one school and added to the collective database. Additional fields would need to be added to the database for recording the location of the owls or other raptors.

Web Links:

Owl Pellets
http://catt.poly.edu/~duane1/zoo/tidbit/owl.html

Lesson Plan—Owl Pellets
http://cybershopping.com/eureka/owl.html

Owl Pellet Activity
http://trms.k12.fulton.ga.net/~dturco/owl-pellet.html

FACTPack Index (Facility for Animal Care and Treatment)
http://www.csubak.edu/fact/FACTPackindex.html

Summary of California studies analyzing the diet of barn owls
http://www.sarep.ucdavis.edu/sarep/newsltr/v7n2/sa-9.htm

Barn Owl
http://www-nais.ccm.emr.ca/schoolnet/issues/risk/birds/ebirds/barnowl.html

The Raptor Center at University. of Minnesota
http://www.raptor.cvm.umn.edu/

Name: _____   Date: _____

ANALYZING OWL PELLETS
SKULL IDENTIFICATION CHART

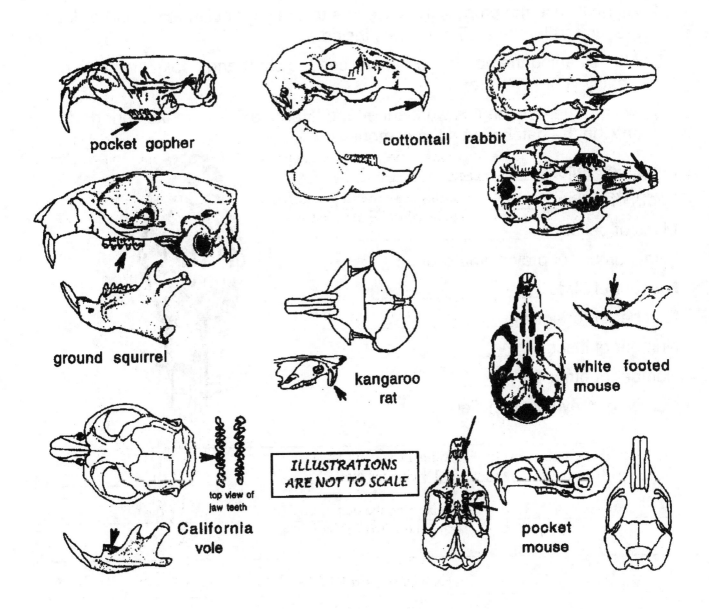

pocket gopher

cottontail rabbit

ground squirrel

kangaroo rat

white footed mouse

top view of jaw teeth

California vole

ILLUSTRATIONS ARE NOT TO SCALE

pocket mouse

Name: _____   Date: _____

ANALYZING OWL PELLETS *(cont.)*

1. Unwrap your pellet.

2. Measure the length and width of your pellet (cm) and record them on this work sheet.

3. Measure the mass of your pellet using the balance scale and record it on this work sheet.

4. Carefully use the probes and tweezers to pull your pellet apart and pick all the fur and feathers off the bones inside.

5. After cleaning the bones thoroughly, use the chart and books available to identify your owl's prey.

6. Record the data on this work sheet and later use this to make your data entry in the database on the computer.

Length of pellet: _____

Width of pellet: _____

Mass of pellet: _____

Total number of prey animals found: _____

Number of birds: _____

Number of rodents: _____

Number of insects: _____

Number of other prey: _____

Names of prey you identified:

_____

_____

_____

_____

_____

_____

BODY SYSTEM SLEUTHS

Start your unit about the human body with a scavenger hunt for body parts. Have the students find their chosen body parts and identify which system they belong to.

Duration:

- 1 or 2 class periods (depending on access to reference materials)

Materials:

- software such as

    Body Works CD-ROM—Softkey

    Total Body CD-ROM—ROMtech

    Inner Body—Informative Graphics

    A.D.A.M. Essentials—A.D.A.M. Software

    InnerBody Works—Tom Snyder

- online access
- body part cards (index cards with body part names written on them)

Before the computer:

- The teacher should make body part cards by using words from the parts list so that each student can pick a part (or several parts).
- Have students put their books away (I'm sure they won't mind!) and have them just use the electronic reference materials.

On the computer:

- Students should research the body part(s) they have chosen.
- They need to find out what body system the part belongs to and what the part does for that system and for the body as a whole.

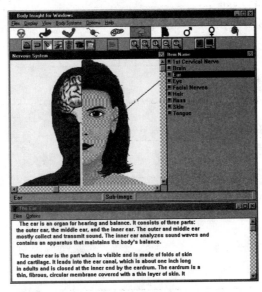

Sample screen from **Body Insight** *by Informative Graphics*

BODY SYSTEM SLEUTHS *(cont.)*

Option:

- Once students have identified all of the body parts, you may want to extend this into a multimedia project. Students can create *HyperStudio* cards or HTML pages for their parts and then link them all together into one whole body project. You can also choose to assign the parts to students as you study each body system and have them create the multimedia project one system at a time. See this project as an example:

The Human Body: The Nervous and Endocrine System
(sample student project)
http://charon.sfsu.edu/school/bodyproj.html

Web Links:

A.D.A.M. Software, Inc.
http://www.adam.com/

The Insight Reference Series
http://www.infograph.com/insight.htm

Inner Body—Human Anatomy Online
http://www.InnerBody.com/

The Visible Human Project
http://www.nlm.nih.gov/research/visible/visible_human.html

LUMEN Structure of Human Body Home Page
Loyola University Medical Education Network
http://www.meddean.luc.edu/lumen/MedEd/GrossAnatomy/GA.html

Colorado State University—Glaxo Virtual Anatomy Project
Virtual Anatomy Image Browser
http://www.vis.colostate.edu/cgi-bin/gva/gvaview

Net-Doctor—Experience Your Body Internet Style
animations of body systems to download
http://www.net-doctor.com/gateway7.html

Science Fact File: Inside the Human Body
http://www.imcpl.lib.in.us/nov_ind.htm

BODY SYSTEM SLEUTHS *(cont.)*

BODY PARTS LIST

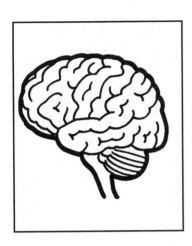
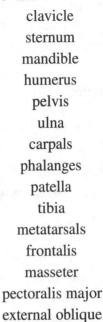
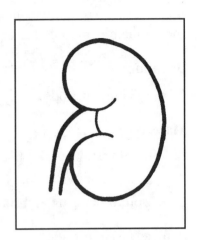

cranium	clavicle
scapula	sternum
maxilla	mandible
vertebra	humerus
rib	pelvis
sacrum	ulna
radius	carpals
metacarpals	phalanges
femur	patella
fibula	tibia
tarsals	metatarsals
temporalis	frontalis
sternomastoid	masseter
deltoid	pectoralis major
biceps	external oblique
sartorius	rectus femoris
vastus lateralis	gastrocnemius
cerebrum	cerebellum
medulla	spinal cord
disk	axon
neuron	dendrite
synapse	pulmonary artery
aorta	vena cava
pulmonary vein	atrium
ventricle	septum
pituitary gland	thyroid gland
parathyroid glands	adrenal glands
pancreas	tongue
epiglottis	larynx
trachea	alveoli
bronchus	bronchioles
lungs	diaphragm
kidney	ureter
nephron	urinary bladder
urethra	salivary glands
esophagus	liver
stomach	gall bladder
small intestine	large intestine
appendix	rectum

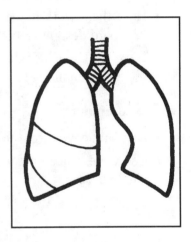
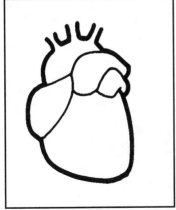
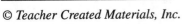
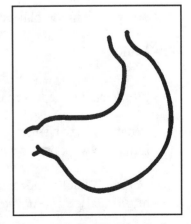

OW! MY WRISTS HURT!

Carpal tunnel syndrome, repetitive stress injury, and ergonomics—are they just buzzwords? Let students find out more about how improper keyboard and mouse use might lead toward wrist injury, and let them work together to try to solve the problem.

Duration:

- 2–3 class periods

Materials:

- reference materials about RTI and carpal tunnel syndrome
- a classroom visit from a local health care professional, if possible
- word processing and simple graphics software

Before the computer:

- Divide class into teams for cooperative activity.
- Have students research RTI and carpal tunnel syndrome—they'll need to know what they are before they can solve the problem.
- Have them work in teams to devise solutions to improper keyboard and mouse use (exercises, new keyboard designs, mouse designs, etc.).
- Have the teams decide how to present their idea(s) to the whole class (descriptive essay, sign, brochure, banner, etc.).

On the computer:

- Use online resources to learn more about RTI and carpal tunnel syndrome.
- Use word processing and graphics software packages to create presentations to be shared with the whole class.

Options:

- You may want to use this lesson to teach the students the exercise techniques and ways to avoid RTI problems and then have them work in teams to create posters, banners, and multimedia presentations about RTI and carpal tunnel syndrome and post them around the school or present them to office personnel.
- Have students create posters about wrist exercises and post them in your computer lab or near computers in the classroom.

Web Links:

Newton's Apple—Carpal Tunnel Syndrome
http://ericir.syr.edu/Projects/Newton/11/carpaltn.html

What Is Carpal Tunnel Syndrome?
http://www.tpcorp.com/macmorran/what.html

Carpal Tunnel Syndrome (CTS)
http://medseek.com/askdrz/pgcts.htm

OW! MY WRISTS HURT! *(cont.)*

Web Links: *(cont.)*

A Patient's Guide to Carpal Tunnel Syndrome
http://www.sechrest.com/mmg/cts/ctsintro.html

American Academy of Orthopedic Surgeons
Exercises may prevent carpal tunnel syndrome
http://www.aaos.org/wordhtml/press/exerci.htm

No Hands Mouse
http://www.hunterdigital.com/tunl_1.htm

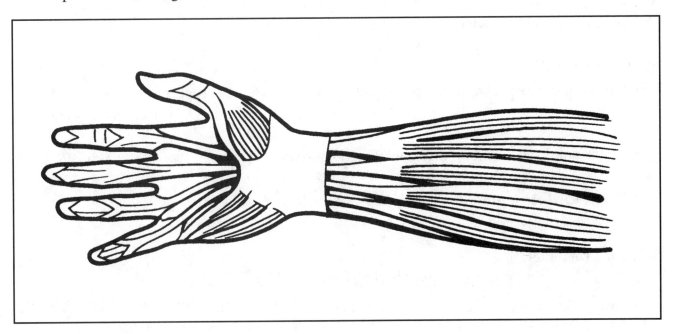

Wrist exercise from the American Academy of Orthopedic Surgeons

1. Hold your arms out in front of your body and extend and stretch the wrists so the hands look like they're in a hand-stand position. Hold that position and count to 5.

2. Allow wrists to straighten and relax.

3. Then, make fists with your hands and bend wrists down. Hold that position and count to 5.

4. Allow wrists to straighten and relax.

Repeat this exercise 10 times and then let arms dangle by your sides and shake them lightly.

MY NOSE KNOWS

The sense of smell is also important in aiding our sense of taste. A study showed that over two million Americans had taste/smell disorders. One such disorder is anosmia—loss of the sense of smell. Use this activity to take the often-used smelling/tasting exercise one step farther and survey your class or school.

Duration:

- 2 class periods to do the lab activity and computer activity with one class
- more time for a school survey—perhaps during lunch periods, other science classes, etc.

Materials:

- plastic bags (for food samples)
- tiny paper cups (for drink samples)
- paper towels
- food samples (carrot, bread, raw potato, onion, apple, celery, green pepper, peanut, pear, mint candy)

  or

- several powdered drink flavors (orange, cherry, grape)

  or

- several jellybean flavors (Buy them as separate flavors at a candy store.)
- spreadsheet software

Before the computer:

- Have students work in pairs with sets of food samples or drink samples.
- Each student will close his/her eyes and try to guess the food or drink first by just smelling it (then by just tasting it, holding nose closed, as well as keeping eyes shut) and then by smelling and tasting it.
- Record correct and incorrect responses on a piece of paper.
- Create a spreadsheet for students to fill in their results.

On computer:

- Fill in a number 1 for each correct guess in the spreadsheet column.
- Have a student (or do this yourself) key in a function command for the spreadsheet program to count all the "ones" in each column.
- Use the totals to create a graph showing the results of the survey (students should see quickly that there were fewer correct responses when only one of the two senses was used).

Option:

- This could be used as an example of surveying techniques for possible science fair projects. Students need to learn how to collect survey data and how to present it so that it actually represents what they are trying to prove.

MY NOSE KNOWS *(cont.)*

	Cherry Smell	Cherry Taste	Cherry Smell & Taste	Orange Smell	Orange Taste	Orange Smell & Taste	Grape Smell	Grape Taste	Grape Smell & Taste
Name									
Kim	1		1		1	1	1		1
Ed		1	1	1		1		1	1
Wayne		1	1	1		1		1	1
Bernadette		1	1					1	1
Jacques	1		1	1		1	1		1
Mike			1		1	1		1	1
Totals									
	Smell	**Taste**	**Smell & Taste**						
Cherry	2	3	6						
Orange	3	2	5						
Grape	2	4	6						

Sample spreadsheet for entering experiment results

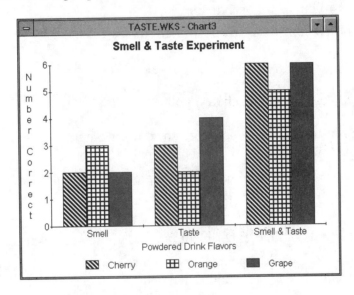

Sample graph to present experiment results

Web Links:

Newton's Apple—Taste and Smell
http://ericir.syr.edu/Projects/Newton/11/tstesmll.html

Smell Taste Disorders
http://www.netdoor.com/entinfo/smellaao.html

Because You Asked About Smell and Taste Disorders
http://www.nih.gov/nidcd/smltaste.htm

Experiments in Good Taste
http://ificinfo.health.org/insight/exper.htm

THE RULER OF REACTION

The study of the nervous system and reflexes is a great time to do this activity about reaction time. It's the standard ruler/yardstick drop/catch lab with extension activities to integrate computer spreadsheets and telecommunications.

Duration:

- portion of a class period for the actual ruler activity
- additional class time for keying information into spreadsheet
- additional classes if you extend this activity into a telecollaboration with other classes via e-mail

Materials:

- metersticks (or rulers) for teams of students, one per pair, if possible (You should be able to convince local hardware or building supply stores to donate them for an educational activity.)
- copies of lab activity instructions for each team
- spreadsheet program (*Microsoft Works, ClarisWorks, AppleWorks*, etc.)

Before the computer:

- Have students complete the lab activity—one student holding/dropping the meterstick and the other catching, and then they switch.
- Have them record their results on the paper work sheet to save until they have the opportunity to enter their results in the spreadsheet.
- The teacher (or a student) creates the spreadsheet template on the computer.

On the computer:

- Students will enter the results of their experiment into the group spreadsheet.
- If you extend this activity to include other classes or other schools via telecommunications, you will need to assign students to key in the additional data.

REACTION.WKS

	A	B	C	D	E	F	G	H	I
1	Name	Sex	Age	R/L	Drop	Drop	Drop	Average	Reaction
2				hand	1	2	3		Time (sec)
3									
4	Laura	f	14	r	11	14	11	12.00	0.16
5	David	m	14	r	11	10	10	10.33	0.15
6	Morag	f	14	r	15	13	9	12.33	0.16
7	Rachel	f	14	l	12	11	12	11.67	0.15
8	Matthew	m	14	r	13	14	10	12.33	0.16
9	Ben	m	14	r	12	12	9	11.00	0.15
10	Rebecca	f	13	r	15	13	9	12.33	0.16
11	Sally	f	14	r	12	12	11	11.67	0.15

Sample of spreadsheet with data entered

THE RULER OF REACTION *(cont.)*

	A	B	C	D	E	F	G	H	I
								REACTION.WKS	
1	Name	Sex	Age	R/L	Drop	Drop	Drop	Average	Reaction
2				hand	1	2	3		Time (sec)
3									
4	Laura	f	14	r	11	14	11	=AVG(E4:G4)	=SQRT(2*H4/981)
5	David	m	14	r	11	10	10	=AVG(E5:G5)	=SQRT(2*H5/981)
6	Morag	f	14	r	15	13	9	=AVG(E6:G6)	=SQRT(2*H6/981)
7	Rachel	f	14	l	12	11	12	=AVG(E7:G7)	=SQRT(2*H7/981)
8	Matthew	m	14	r	13	14	10	=AVG(E8:G8)	=SQRT(2*H8/981)
9	Ben	m	14	r	12	12	9	=AVG(E9:G9)	=SQRT(2*H9/981)
10	Rebecca	f	13	r	15	13	9	=AVG(E10:G10)	=SQRT(2*H10/981)
11	Sally	f	14	r	12	12	11	=AVG(E11:G11)	=SQRT(2*H11/981)

View of spreadsheet showing formulas for average and reaction time

Options:

- Extend this activity so that each student tests his/her reaction time with both hands and then creates a simple spreadsheet and graphs the contrast between hands. Have students use the "Comparing Ambidexterity" work sheet.

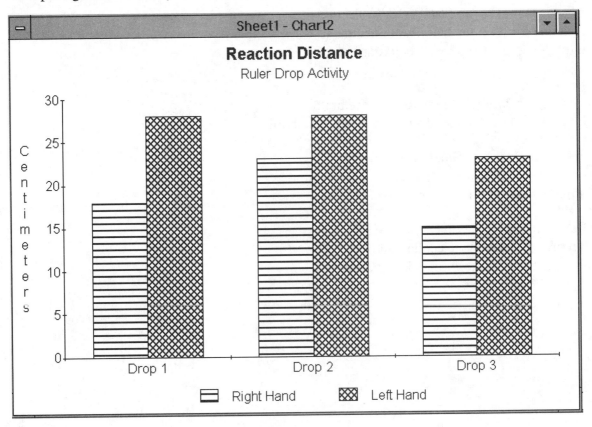

- Use this activity to compare boys' reaction times with girls' reaction times or right-handed students vs. left-handed students. (Hopefully, the results will be similar in both sets of groups so that you'll have an opportunity to dispel a few more myths about generalizations.)

THE RULER OF REACTION *(cont.)*

Options: *(cont.)*

- Have students measure their parents' reaction times and compare students' vs. parents' speeds.
- Test the whole school. Test other schools in your area or use this as a telecommunications activity. In the back of this book, you will find locations where you can post a telecollaborative activity, and hopefully other teachers will do the same lab and send you their results. Offer to post all the results on a Web page or at least e-mail all the results to all participating teachers.

Web Links:

Neuroscience for Kids—information and additional activities—
activity "How Fast Are You?" and a reaction time conversion chart
http://Weber.u.washington.edu/~chudler/neurok.html

Testing Reaction Times
http://www.shu.ac.uk/schools/sci/sol/invest/react_1/react.htm

Newton's Apple—Reflexes
http://www.ktca.org/newtons/13/rlxes.html

Wisconsin/Michigan State Brain Collections
A Gallery of Mammalian Brain Specimens
http://www.neurophys.wisc.edu/brain

Brain Poke
Learn the anatomy and function of the brain.
http://www.circ.uab.edu/BrainPoke/BrainPoke.html

Test Your Reaction Time!
Online reaction time test page
http://www.forerunners.com/RT.HTM

Reaction Time Experiment
Archive of a sample telecollaborative project
http://archives.gsn.org/sept95/0020.html

THE RULER OF REACTION *(cont.)*

REACTION TIME CONVERSION CHART

Average	Reaction Time (sec)
1	0.05
2	0.06
3	0.08
4	0.09
5	0.10
6	0.11
7	0.12
8	0.13
9	0.14
10	0.14
11	0.15
12	0.16
13	0.16
14	0.17
15	0.17
16	0.18
17	0.19
18	0.19
19	0.20
20	0.20
21	0.21
22	0.21
23	0.22
24	0.22
25	0.23
26	0.23
27	0.23
28	0.24
29	0.24
30	0.25

Note:

Conversions are calculated using this formula:

(Reaction time [sec]) = Square Root {2 x (Drop Length [cm]) / 981}

$$R = \sqrt{\frac{2 * L}{981}}$$

Name: _____   Date_____

THE RULER OF REACTION

LAB ACTIVITY

Hold the meterstick up in the air so it is hanging down from your fingers. Have your partner hold his or her fingers just under the bottom of the meterstick.

Tell your partner you will let go of the meterstick some time in the next 5 seconds and he or she must attempt to catch it as quickly as possible.

Record the number of centimeters that passed by your partner's hands before he or she caught the meterstick. Repeat this two more times and record all measurements.

Switch places and let your partner hold and drop the meterstick for you to catch.

Record all of your measurements on this page.

Save this paper to input the measurements into the spreadsheet when you work on the computer.

Name:_____

Sex: F   M   Age: _____   Hand: L   R

Attempt   Measurement

  1. _____

  2. _____

  3. _____

Name:_____

Sex: F   M   Age: _____   Hand: L   R

Attempt   Measurement

  1. _____

  2. _____

  3. _____

Name: _____   Date_____

THE RULER OF REACTION
COMPARING AMBIDEXTERITY

Hold the meterstick up in the air so it is hanging down from your fingers. Have your partner hold his or her fingers just under the bottom of the meterstick.

Tell your partner you will let go of the meterstick some time in the next 5 seconds and he or she must attempt to catch it as quickly as possible with his or her dominant hand.

Record the number of centimeters that passed by your partner's hands before he or she caught the meterstick. Repeat this two more times and record all measurements. Have your partner use the hand not normally used, and repeat the experiment and record the measurements.

Switch places and let your partner hold and drop the meterstick for you to catch.

Record all of your measurements on this page, also.

Save this paper to input the measurements into the spreadsheet when you work on the computer.

Name:_____

Sex: F   M   Age: _____   Dominant Hand: L   R

Attempt	Dominant Hand Measurement	Other Hand Measurement
1.	_____	_____
2.	_____	_____
3.	_____	_____

Name:_____

Sex: F   M   Age: _____   Dominant Hand: L   R

Attempt	Dominant Hand Measurement	Other Hand Measurement
1.	_____	_____
2.	_____	_____
3.	_____	_____

WHAT'S THAT TREE?

This is a great way to use technology to extend the old, standard leaf collection projects.

Duration:

- Give students adequate time to collect tree information to input into their databases.
- Use this as an ongoing class project about trees in your area.
- If this is an individual project, students should be given ample time to identify specimens, and they should be able to enter data on the computer in one class period.

Materials:

- tree identification reference materials (books, CD-ROM, online access)
- work sheets about tree identification and leaf identification (These could be enlarged and mounted as posters for an ongoing project.)
- database software (*Microsoft Works*, *ClarisWorks*, *AppleWorks*, etc.)

Before the computer:

- Copy tree identification materials and either use them as posters or handouts.
- Have students identify common trees and have information ready to input into a database.
- Create a database template for students to use.

On the computer:

- Students will input data entries about identified trees.

Option:

- You may want to use this information to extend the activity to incorporate a multimedia project by some or all of the students. A digital camera or scanner would be very helpful at this point if you wanted to include photos of the trees and leaves.

Part 1 of sample database for entering tree data

	Common Name	Genus	Species	Tree Shape	Leaf Arrange.	Leaf Type	Leaf S
1							
2							
3							
4							
5							
6							
7							
8							

TREES.WDB

WHAT S THAT TREE? *(cont.)*

	Leaf Type	Leaf Shape	Leaf Apex	Leaf Base	Leaf Edges	Leaf Veins	Fruit Type	Flower Typ
1								
2								
3								
4								
5								
6								
7								
8								
9								
10								
11								

TREES.WDB

Part 2 of sample database for entering tree data

Web Links:

Iowa State University Extension—Identification of Native Trees of Iowa
http://www.exnet.iastate.edu/Pages/tree/

Tree Classification
http://www.america.net/~toms/class1.htm

Tree Identification
http://www.america.net/~toms/ident.htm

Youth Science Forum—World Leaf Collection
Add your local leaves to the online collection of data and photos.
http://www.vpds.wsu.edu/SciForum/

Oregon State University—Trees of the Pacific Northwest
online dichotomous key and mystery tree identification game
http://www.orst.edu/instruct/for241/

Arbor Day—125 Years of Tradition
http://www.arborday.com/

University of Wisconsin-Madison's Virtual Foliage Home Page
http://www.wisc.edu/botany/virtual.html

Tree Book—Learning to Recognize Trees of British Columbia
http://www.for.gov.bc.ca/pab/EDUCATE/TREEBOOK/tree-toc.htm

Common Wild Plants of the C & O Canal
searchable database
http://fledge.watson.org/rivendell/botany-db/

WHAT'S THAT TREE? *(cont.)*

Tree Shape

Broad (horizontal oval)
Columnar
Conical
Pyramidal
Rounded
Umbrella
Upright Oval
Vase
Weeping

Leaf Arrangement

Alternate
Opposite
Whorled
Compound—Pinnate
Compound—Bi-Pinnate

Leaf Type

Simple
Compound—Trifolate
Compound—Palmate

Leaf Shape

Awl-like
Cordate
Deltoid
Elliptic
Lanceolate
Linear
Needle-like
Oblanceolate
Oblong
Obovate
Oval
Ovate
Rhomboid
Scale-like
Spatulate

Leaf Apex (tip)

Acuminate
Acute
Cuspidate
Emarginate
Mucronate
Obtuse
Round
Truncate

Leaf Base

Acute
Auriculate
Cordate
Cuneate
Inequilateral
Obtuse
Round
Truncate

Leaf Edges

Deep Lobed
Dentate
Double Serrate
Entire
Lobed
Revolute
Serrate
Undulate

Leaf Veins

Parallel
Pinnate
Palmate
Arcuate

Fruit Types

Achenes
Berries
Capsules
Cones
Drupes
Follicles
Legumes
Nut with Husk
Pume
Samaras

Flower Types

Catkin
Corymb
Cyme
Flat-Head
Globose
Panicle
Raceme
Spike
Umbel

STUDENT HYDROLOGISTS

There are many indicators of water quality in our lakes and rivers. These activities will provide students with the opportunity to collect real data and possibly compare/contrast their data with that collected by students in other schools—along the same body of water or in different locations.

Duration:

- should be developed as a comparative year-long study

Materials:

Minimum materials should include the following:

- thermometers
- water quality test kits (pH and dissolved oxygen)
- beakers
- droppers

Additional materials should include the following:

- test kits for pH, dissolved oxygen, phosphate, nitrite/nitrate, ammonia, copper, lead, fecal coliform
- wind speed and direction indicator
- Secchi discs

Ideally, materials will include the following:

- sensors and probeware for computer or CBL (Calculator Based Laboratory) (manufactured by Texas Instruments, Vernier, or Team Labs)
- database software
- telecommunications access—for sharing of data

Before the computer:

- Contact teachers at other schools in your area or other schools around the state, country, or world via e-mail to participate in sharing your data collection and comparison activity.
- Join a collaborative online project or start one of your own by using a Web site to post collected data (see suggestions below).
- Students should have a basic knowledge of river/lake environments and the impact of water quality on life forms there.
- Perform exploratory exercises to learn how to use test kits or sensors and probeware.

  Dissolved oxygen levels of less than 5.0 mg/l put fish under stress.

  Using a dissolved oxygen test kit, measure the dissolved oxygen in the water at your collection site.

STUDENT HYDROLOGISTS (cont.)

Before the computer: (*cont.*)

For aquatic life, pH levels should be between 6.0 and 9.0.

Using pH test strips, a liquid test kit, or probeware, measure the water pH at your collection site.

---

pH Table

pH Level	Effect
3.0–3.5	Fish will survive for only a few hours.
3.5–4.0	Trout and salmon will die.
4.0–4.5	Fish eggs will not hatch.
5.0–5.5	Plankton die; sediment metals are released into the water.
6.0–6.5	Some freshwater crustaceans will die.
6.5–8.0	These are favorable conditions.
8.0–9.0	Not harmful, but chemical reactions in water may be affected.
9.0–10.5	Long exposure is harmful to salmon, trout, and other species.
10.5–11.0	Salmon, trout, and perch will die.
11.0 +	All fish will eventually die.

STUDENT HYDROLOGISTS *(cont.)*

On the computer:

- Create a database which includes these fields:

Site	Cloud Cover
Teacher	Rain
Location	Air Temp
Date	Water Temp
Time	Water Color
Wind Direction	pH
Wind Speed	Dissolved Oxygen

and all other fields for which you will be collecting data

- Use test kits or probeware or CBL to collect data on a regular basis. Involve volunteers to assist you by helping a weekly team of students go to the collection site and gather data after the entire class has been instructed on how to use the equipment.

- If using probeware or CBL equipment, create graphs of weekly data and post it on a bulletin board for class viewing and comparison.

- If collaborating with one or more other classes, collect data in a timely fashion and report back to them with your data, as well.

- Create a Web page, either on a school server or at one of the free home page services online, for reporting and archiving weekly data.

Options:

- If possible, take a digital photo or regular photo and scan it into a digital image and archive it with the data. Extend the Web page process to include uploading the image for other school participants to view. This would be a good archive of visual data from the collection site.

- If students find a potential ecological hazard, assist them in informing the proper authorities and requesting updates on the solution to the problem.

- Tom Snyder Productions' *Decisions, Decisions: The Environment* is an interactive critical thinking program about making decisions about how to control pollution in a local landfill. Students act as the mayor of the town and are guided by experts with opinions as to how to save the environment and win the upcoming election. You can use this to extend the concept of water quality since pollution in a town landfill could potentially leach through the soil and into the city's water supply.

STUDENT HYDROLOGISTS *(cont.)*

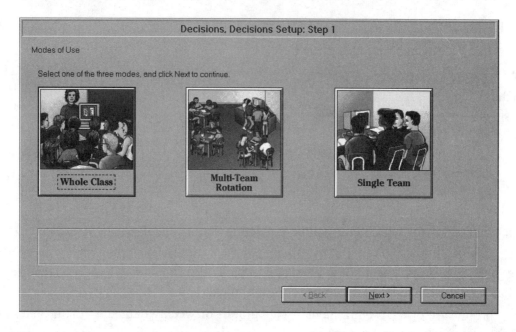

Reprinted with permission from Tom Snyder Productions

All of the *Decisions, Decisions* software packages are designed to be used with whole classes, teams within the class, or small team interaction. The decision is made when starting the program each time you use it.

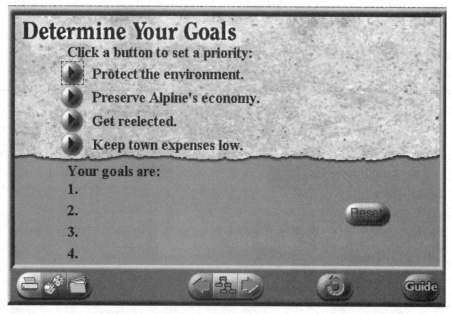

Reprinted with permission from Tom Snyder Productions

Acting as the mayor, students must begin the program by prioritizing the four main goals they must accomplish as they continue.

STUDENT HYDROLOGISTS *(cont.)*

Reprinted with permission from Tom Snyder Productions

Throughout the program, students must make decisions based on information they receive from their various advisors and from researching their booklets.

The discussions that begin with the use of this program can also be taken online if you have Internet access in your school or classroom. There are instructions given for joining the online discussion group in the teacher handbook.

Web Links:

Sensors, Probeware, and Calculator Based Laboratory Web Sites

Vernier Sensors and Probes and Calculator Based Laboratory
http://www.vernier.com

Texas Instruments—Calculator Based Laboratory
http://www.ti.com/calc/docs/cbl.htm

Programs for TI-Calculators and CBL (Calculator Based Laboratory)
http://www.vernier.com/cbl/progs.html

Team Labs: Personal Science Laboratory
http://www.teamlabs.com/

Access Excellence—Technology in Education—Probeware
http://www.gene.com/ae/21st/TE/PW/

STUDENT HYDROLOGISTS *(cont.)*

Web Links: *(cont.)*

Water Quality and Collaborative Projects Web Sites

Hydrology-Related Internet Resources
http://terrassa.pnl.gov:2080/EESC/resourcelist/hydrology.html

Access Excellence—Technology in Education—Probeware
http://www.gene.com/ae/21st/TE/PW/

The GLOBE Project—International Hands-On Science and Education
Global Learning and Observations to Benefit the Environment
http://www.globe.gov/

GREEN—Global Rivers Environmental Education Network
http://www.igc.apc.org/green/green.html

Rivers Online
http://rol.freenet.columbus.oh.us/index.html

Texas Rivers Distance Learning Project
http://chico.rice.edu/armadillo/Ftbend/rivers.html

Free Web Page Hosting

Geocities
http://www.geocities.com

Tripod
http://www.tripod.com

Angelfire
http://www.angelfire.com

BIOME, SWEET BIOME

Areas with similar climate, plants, and animals have been classified by scientists as biomes. The major biomes are grassland, desert, tundra, taiga—coniferous forest, temperate—deciduous forest, tropical rain forest, and aquatic (marine and freshwater). Have your students find out about biomes through these activities.

Duration:

- several class periods for research and creating displays/projects

Materials:

- reference works about biomes/ecology (books, videotapes, software, online access)
- biome software such as:

  The Great Ocean Rescue—Tom Snyder Productions

  Rainforest Researchers—Tom Snyder Productions

  EcoMaster—Cascoly Software
- database software
- multimedia planning sheet
- sign-making/presentation/multimedia software (*The Print Shop, HyperStudio, Netscape Navigator*, etc.)

Before the computer:

- Divide the class into groups and assign each group one biome or assign each member within each group a biome.
- Have students use research materials to find out what climate, flora, and fauna are in their biome.

On the computer:

- Have teams prepare presentations to share their information with the rest of the class.

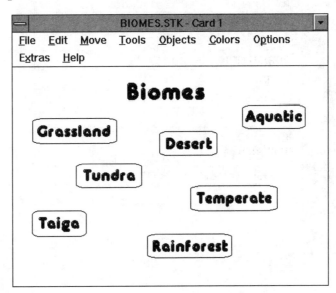

Index screen for multimedia presentation—created using **HyperStudio**

BIOME, SWEET BIOME *(cont.)*

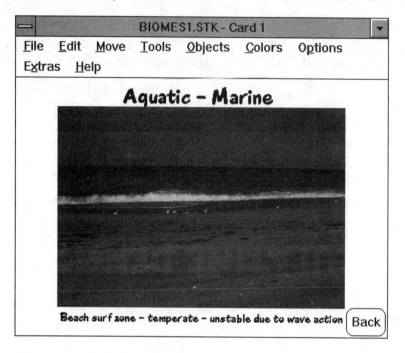

Sample card within multimedia presentation

Options:

- Have students keep a database of organisms and biomes which they will add to as you study each of the biomes.

	Organism	Biome	
1	Bay Scallops	Aquatic	
2	Birch	Temperate	
3	Bison	Grassland	
4	Eelgrass	Aquatic	
5	Elk	Taiga	
6	Green Turtle	Aquatic	
7	Hemlock	Temperate	
8	Lemmings	Tundra	
9	Lynx	Tundra	
10	Mule Deer	Taiga	
11	Prairie Dogs	Grassland	
12	Snowshoe Hare	Taiga	
13	Spruce	Taiga	
14			

Sample database file

BIOME, SWEET BIOME *(cont.)*

Options: *(cont.)*

- Students could keep a different database that shows that some organisms or groups of organisms may be found in more than one biome in the world. They could edit the database as you study each of the biomes and learn about more organisms. You could keep the "Organism" column simple or add fields to the database for specific organism name and scientific name.

	Organism	Grassland	Desert	Tundra	Taiga	Temperate	Rainforest	Marine
1	Phytoplankton							yes
2	Raccoons				yes	yes		
3	Flounder							yes
4	Moss			yes	yes	yes		
5	Lichen			yes	yes	yes		
6								

(Data2)

Sample database file

- In *EcoMaster*—a game for Windows—students bid on and trade different animals according to their abilities to thrive in different biomes (available from Cascoly Software—the shareware version limited, additional animals and biomes in registered version).

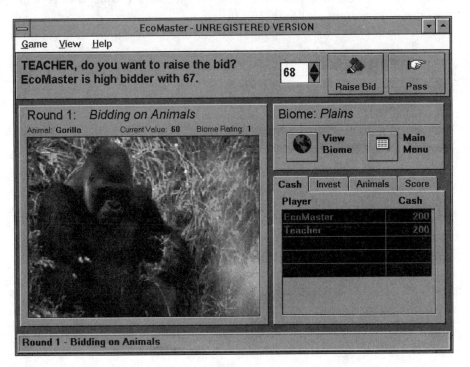

Sample screen from EcoMaster

BIOME, SWEET BIOME *(cont.)*

Options: *(cont.)*

- If you have online access available, have students work in pairs to find additional Web sites about the different biomes. Give them the task of finding five links. Each link should meet the following criteria:

    It should be a complete and valid URL (Universal Resource Locator).

    Each Web site should come from a different biome type.

    The site should have a good picture or graphic showing at least one organism in the biome.

    It should include a short description of the Web site along with the URL—about the organisms or about that biome type.

- You can then post all of the URLs reported to you on a poster near your computer with online access, and students can use those sites as reference materials for their other projects.

- If you have e-mail access, you can start a collaborative project via the Internet and list it with Global SchoolNet. One such project involved students e-mailing a class about their lives in various biomes of the world. Survey questions were posted by members of the class in order to help them study the flora, fauna, geography, natural resources, climate, and explorers of the major biomes. The survey included the following questions:

    What kind of clothes do you wear?

    What is the weather like where you live?

    What kinds of homes do you have?

- The complete activity can be found in the Global SchoolNet's project archives at this Web address: http://archives.gsn.org/oct96/0043.html.

Web Links:

The World's Biomes
http://www.ucmp.berkeley.edu/glossary/gloss5/biome/

Missouri Botanical Gardens—Virtual Biomes
http://www.mobot.org/MBGnet/vb/index.htm

Marlborough's Biomes Page (Resources on biomes)
http://www.marlborough.la.ca.us/depts/science/biomes.html

EcoMaster—Cascoly Software
http://cascoly.com/eco.htm

Global SchoolNet's Internet Projects Registry
http://www.gsn.org/gsn/proj/index.html

MULTIMEDIA PLANNING SHEET

Title Card

Buttons/Links: _____

Notes (Text/Sounds/Animations): _____

Card 1

Buttons/Links: _____

Notes (Text/Sounds/Animations): _____

Card 2

Buttons/Links: _____

Notes (Text/Sounds/Animations): _____

Card 3

Buttons/Links: _____

Notes (Text/Sounds/Animations): _____

Card 4

Buttons/Links: _____

Notes (Text/Sounds/Animations): _____

Card 5

Buttons/Links: _____

Notes (Text/Sounds/Animations): _____

STRUGGLING TO SURVIVE

In 1973, Congress passed the Endangered Species Act in an effort to identify those species which were threatened by economic growth and development of land areas and to provide a program for the conservation of those species. This activity will provide your students an opportunity to find out if we have improved our environment significantly in the last 20 years.

Duration:

- class time for research in library or online
- additional home time for more research—depending on your local resources
- time for students to write to various organizations to ask them about the status of some of the animals

Materials:

- reference materials (current CD-ROM encyclopedias, online access, periodicals such as national and state wildlife magazines, museum curators, etc.)
- several copies of the Endangered and Threatened Species Lists from 1973 for students to look at while they choose an animal

    or

- overhead transparencies of the lists for students to choose animals

Before the computer:

- Using online or book resources, teach about the Endangered Species Act of 1973. You will find several Web links which contain copies of the Act as well as some which have explanations/translations.
- Have each student pick an animal from the 1973 lists.
- Talk to students about reliability of resources and about how current some of those resources are.
- Go to your school library and research in reference books and periodicals to find the animal's current status.

On the computer:

- Use current CD-ROM encyclopedia or science reference software and/or online access to the Internet to research the animal's current status.
- Current Status should be listed as follows:

    extinct

    rare

    endangered

    threatened

    vulnerable

    off the lists because they have made a comeback.

STRUGGLING TO SURVIVE *(cont.)*

Options:

- If you have online access in your room, have students view the slide show "Endangered Means There's Still Time!" at the U.S. Fish & Wildlife Service Web site.
- Have class discussion about how our environment has changed in the past 20+ years. Obtain a current Endangered & Threatened Species List and contrast the numbers of organisms on the past and current lists. Be sure students are aware of the number of new listings.
- If time allows, have students find more information about their animals and report to the class. This could tie in with a study of biomes and ecological niches.

Web Links:

Endangered Species Home Page, U.S. Fish & Wildlife Service
http://www.fws.gov/~r9endspp/endspp.html

Endangered Species Act Online Resource Guide
http://www.envirolink.org/issues/esa/

Endangered Species Act of 1973
http://www.usbr.gov/laws/esa.html
or
http://kingfish.ssp.nmfs.gov/tmcintyr/esahome.html

The Middlebury College Endangered Species Home Page
http://www.middlebury.edu/~classadm/bi423/

National Wildlife Federation
http://www.nwf.org/nwf/

National Wildlife Federation System
http://bluegoose.arw.r9.fws.gov/

Federal Wildlife Laws and Governing Agencies
http://www.bev.net/education/SeaWorld/endangered_species/esIV.html

EE-Link Endangered Species
http://www.nceet.snre.umich.edu/EndSpp/Endangered.html

Endangered Species
http://www.nceet.snre.umich.edu/EndSpp/Endangered.html

From Alligators to Whooping Cranes
http://riceinfo.rice.edu/armadillo/Endanger/about.html

STRUGGLING TO SURVIVE *(cont.)*

ENDANGERED SPECIES—1973

MAMMALS

Bat, Hawaiian Hoary
Bat, Indiana
Cougar, Eastern
Deer, Columbian W. Tailed
Deer, Key
Ferret, Black-Footed
Fox, San Joaquin Kit
Manatee, Florida
Mouse, Salt Marsh Harvest
Panther, Florida
Prairie Dog, Utah
Pronghorn, Sonoran
Rat, Morro Bay Kangaroo
Squirrel, Delmarva Fox
Whale, Blue
Whale, Bowhead
Whale, Finback
Whale, Gray
Whale, Humpback
Whale, Right
Whale, Sei
Whale, Sperm
Wolf, Eastern Timber
Wolf, N. Rocky Mountain
Wolf, Red

REPTILES & AMPHIBIANS

Alligator, American
Lizard, Blunt-Nosed Leopard
Salamander, Desert Slender
Salamander, Santa Cruz Long-Toed
Snake, San Francisco Garter

FISHES

Bonytail, Pahranagat
Chub, Humpback
Chub, Mohave
Cisco, Longjaw
Cui-Ui
Dace, Kendall Warm Springs
Dace, Moapa
Darter, Fountain
Darter, Maryland
Darter, Okaloosa
Darter, Watercress
Gambusia, Big Bend
Gambusia, Clear Creek
Gambusia, Pecos
Killifish, Pahrump
Pike, Blue
Pupfish, Comanche Springs
Pupfish, Devils Hole
Pupfish, Owens River
Pupfish, Tecopa
Pupfish, Warm Spring
Squawfish, Colorado River
Stickleback, Unarmored Threespine
Sturgeon, Shortnose
Topminnow, Gila
Trout, Arizona
Trout, Gila
Trout, Greenback Cutthroat
Trout, Paiute Cutthroat
Trout, Lahontan Cutthroat
Woundfin

STRUGGLING TO SURVIVE *(cont.)*

ENDANGERED SPECIES—1973

BIRDS

Akepa, Hawaii

Akepa, Maui

Akialoa, Kauai

Akiapolaau

Bobwhite, Masked

Condor, California

Coot, Hawaiian

Crane, Mississippi Sandhill

Crane, Whooping

Creeper, Molokai

Creeper, Oahu

Crow, Hawaiian

Curlew, Eskimo

Duck, Hawaiian

Duck, Laysan

Duck, Mexican

Eagle, Southern Bald

Falcon, Am. Peregrine

Falcon, Arctic Peregrine

Finches, Laysan and Nihoa

Gallinule, Hawaiian

Goose, Aleutian Canada

Goose, Hawaiian

Hawk, Hawaiian

Honeycreeper, Crested

Kite, Florida Everglade

Millerbird, Nihoa

Nukupuus, Kauai and Maui

Oo, Kauai

Ou

Palila

Parrot, Puerto Rican

Parrotbill, Maui

Pelican, Brown

Petrel, Hawaiian Dark-rumped

Pigeon, Puerto Rican Plain

Prairie Chicken, Attwater's Greater

Rail, California Clapper

Rail, Light-footed Clapper

Rail, Yuma Clapper

Sparrow, Cape Sable

Sparrow, Dusky Seaside

Sparrow, Santa Barbara Song

Stilt, Hawaiian

Tern, California Least

Thrush, Large Kauai

Thrush, Molokai

Thrush, Small Kauai

Warbler, Bachman's

Warbler, Kirtland's

Whippoorwill, P. R.

Woodpecker, Ivory-Billed

Woodpecker, Red-Cockaded

STRUGGLING TO SURVIVE *(cont.)*

THREATENED SPECIES—1973

MAMMALS

Bat, Ozark Big-Eared
Bat, Spotted
Bat, Virginia Big-Eared
Bear, Glacier
Bighorn, California
Bighorn, Peninsular
Elk, Tule
Rat, Key Largo Wood
Sea Otter, Southern
Seal, Caribbean Monk
Seal, Guadalupe Fur
Seal, Hawaiian Monk
Seal, Ribbon
Squirrel, Everglades Fox
Squirrel, Kaibab
Vole, Beach Meadow
Vole, Block Island Meadow
Wolf, Mexican

BIRDS

Crane, Florida Sandhill
Falcon, Prairie
Finch, Wallowa Gray-Crowned Rosy
Goose, Tule White-Fronted
Hawk, P. R. Sharp-Shinned
Heron, Florida Great White
Owl, Newton's Puerto Rican Screech
Owl, Spotted
Prairie Chicken, Lesser
Prairie Chicken, Northern Greater
Rail, California Black
Shearwater, Newell's Manx
Sparrow, Ipswich
Warbler, Elfin Woods
Warbler, Golden-Cheeked

FISHES

Bass, Roanoke
Bass, Suwannee
Cavefish, Ozark
Cisco, Blackfin
Cisco, Deepwater
Dace, Desert
Darter, Niangua
Darter, Sharphead
Darter, Trispot
Darter, Tuscumbia
Gambusia, San Marcos
Grayling, Arctic
Mudminnow, Olympic
Pupfish, Nevada
Sculpin, Pygmy
Spinedace, Little Colorado
Sturgeon, Lake
Sucker, Murdoc
Sucker, White River
Trout, Blueback
Trout, Humboldt Cutthroat
Trout, Little Kern Golden
Trout, Rio Grande Cutthroat
Trout, Sunapee

REPTILES & AMPHIBIANS

Crocodile, American
Frog, Pine Barrens Tree
Frog, Vegas Valley Leopard
Lizard, St. Croix Ground
Salamander, Jemez Mountain
Salamander, Limestone
Salamander, Shasta
Salamander, Tehachapi Slender
Toad, Black
Turtle, Bog
Turtle, Green

IT'S ELEMENTAL

Students will use electronic periodic tables to calculate numbers of protons, neutrons, and electrons. They will also be able to search for additional data about the elements, depending on the program or online source.

Duration:

- 1 class period

Materials:

- copies of a blank periodic table of elements
- periodic table software
- online access

Before the computer:

- The teacher should review the parts of a periodic table and what data the students will find on the software available.

On the computer:

- After picking 10 elements, use the software or online periodic table to fill in the blanks on the work sheet.
- Use the calculator program to compute numbers of protons, neutrons, and electrons for each element chosen.

Option:

- Depending on the software or online access available, you could add items to the list for students to research. Several of the programs include quite a lot of data about each element. You could also create a database template and choose fields for which the students can find data.

Web Links:

Periodic Table of the Elements
http://kufacts.cc.ukans.edu/cwis/reference/Periodic/periodic.html

Web Elements
http://www.shcf.ac.uk/uni/academic/A-C/chem/Web-elements/Web-elements-home.html

The Pictorial Periodic Table
http://chemlab.pc.maricopa.edu/periodic/periodic.html

Chemicool Periodic Table
http://the-tech.mit.edu/Chemicool/

The Periodic Table of Elements on the Internet
http://domains.twave.net/domain/yinon/default.html

Shareware download site (This site has Mac and Windows software available.)
http://www.shareware.com

IT'S ELEMENTAL *(cont.)*

Downloadable Programs for Windows:

The Periodic Table for Windows—Winpte
shareware program—30-day evaluation period
http://anders.compart.fi/winpte
created by 16-year-old Anders Lindh of Finland

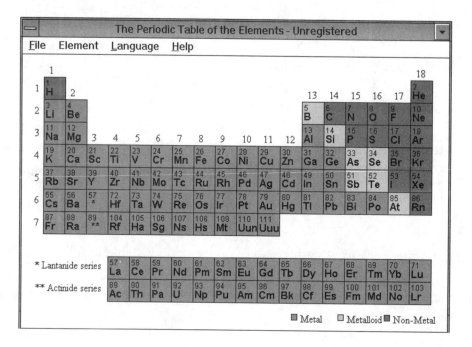

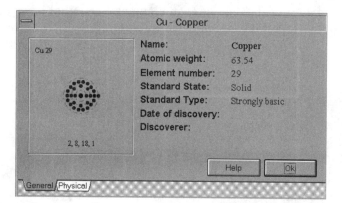

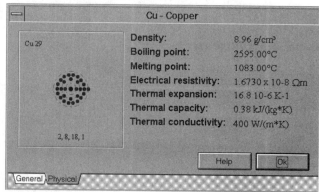

IT'S ELEMENTAL *(cont.)*

Periodic Table (element3.exe)
freeware for Windows
http://www.shareware.com (search for periodic table)
created by Gregory Jones and Charles Perrin

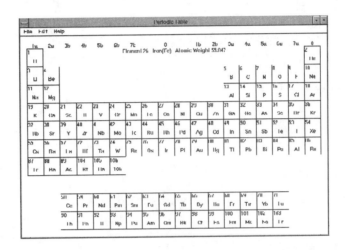

BK Periodic Library
freeware to students to use on home computers
$30 licensing fee for school computer use
http://bk.base.org/perlib
created by Billy Klein

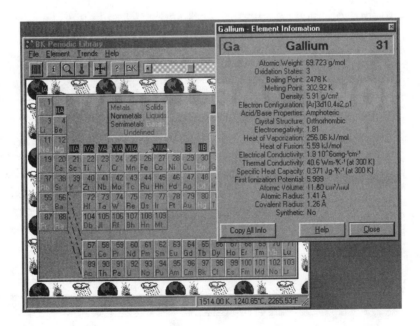

CALCULATING DENSITY

Students will use data collected in a lab activity and create a simple spreadsheet and graph to illustrate their findings. This is good practice before science projects are due.

Duration:

- 1 class period in science lab
- 1 class period on computer

Materials:

- 5–10 objects to measure volumes
- graduated cylinders
- water
- balance scales
- work sheet—"Calculating Density"
- spreadsheet program (*Microsoft Works, ClarisWorks, AppleWorks*, etc.)

Before the computer:

- Collect sets of small items for each lab group—piece of chalk, small rock, paper clip, game piece, etc., and make sure they are small enough to fit in the graduated cylinders.
- Students should measure the masses of their objects on a balance scale (in grams).
- Students will partially fill a graduated cylinder with water to 10 ml or 20 ml.
- Have them drop the items (one at a time) into the water and record the difference in water level as the volume of the object in ml (or cm^3).
- They should record this collected data on the work sheet "Calculating Density."

	A	B	C	D	E
1	Object	Mass m (g)	Volume v (mL)	Density d=m/v (g/mL)	
2					
3	item one	5	2.5	2.00	
4	item two	6	7.5	0.80	
5	item three	3	3.9	0.77	
6	item four	9	6.1	1.48	

DENSITY1.WKS

Sample spreadsheet showing number values

CALCULATING DENSITY *(cont.)*

	A	B	C	D	E
1	Object	Mass m (g)	Volume v (mL)	Density d=m/v (g/mL	
2					
3	item one	5	2.5	=B3/C3	
4	item two	6	7.5	=B4/C4	
5	item three	3	3.9	=B5/C5	
6	item four	9	6.1	=B6/C6	
7					
8					
9					
10					

DENSITY1.WKS

Sample spreadsheet showing formula for density

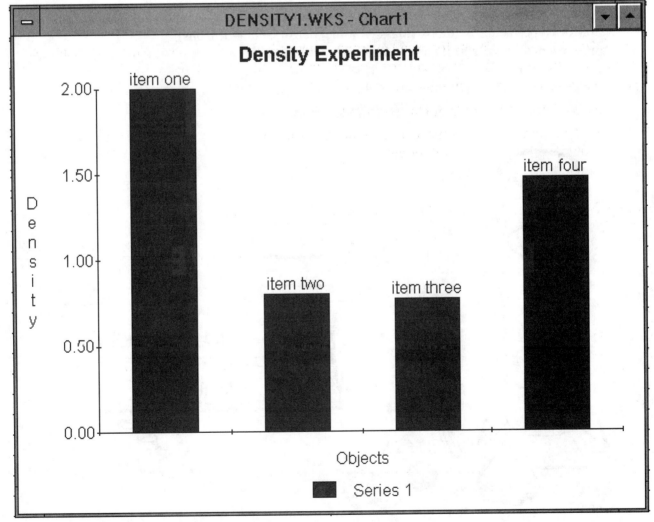

Sample graph of calculated densities

CALCULATING DENSITY *(cont.)*

On the computer:

- Have students create the spreadsheet and fill in the data for mass and volume (make sure they only key in the numbers in the cells on the spreadsheet).
- Have students create a bar graph of the density results and label the graph (according to the instructions of your spreadsheet software).

Options:

- If you don't have access to a computer lab, you could have each team use the computer to create their spreadsheets and graphs. Make sure the team signs the project for grading purposes.
- You could extend this activity to a lesson about reliability of data collection by comparing/contrasting the density calculations of each team.

Web Links:

MathMol—Mathematics and Molecules
http://www.nyu.edu/pages/mathmol/

MathMol Hypermedia Textbook (mass, volume, density, etc.—lessons)
http://www.nyu.edu/pages/mathmol/textbook/middle_home.html

Density—Science Museum of Minnesota
http://www.sci.mus.mn.us/sln/tf/d/density/density.html

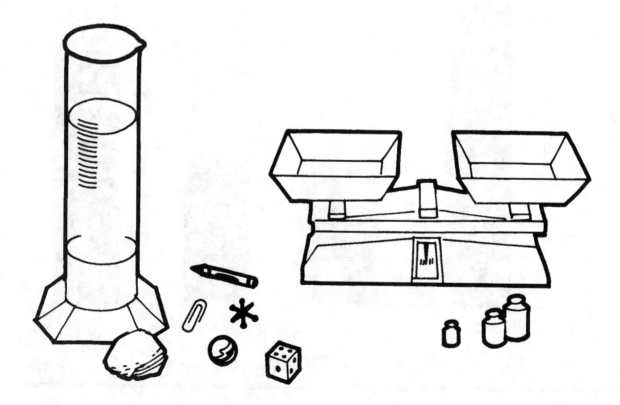

Name: _____　Date: _____

CALCULATING DENSITY

1. Write the names of each of the objects or substances in the first column.

2. Using a balance scale, measure the mass of each object and record the measurement (in grams) in the second column.

3. Measure the volume of each object by using the graduated cylinder. Fill the cylinder with water to the 10 ml mark. Place the object in the cylinder and calculate the difference in volume as the volume of the object. Record this measurement (in ml) in the third column.

4. You will create a spreadsheet on the computer to determine the density of each of the objects. After completing that activity, record the results in the fourth column of this sheet.

Substance	Mass	Volume	Density
_____	_____	_____	_____
_____	_____	_____	_____
_____	_____	_____	_____
_____	_____	_____	_____
_____	_____	_____	_____
_____	_____	_____	_____
_____	_____	_____	_____
_____	_____	_____	_____
_____	_____	_____	_____
_____	_____	_____	_____
_____	_____	_____	_____
_____	_____	_____	_____
_____	_____	_____	_____

ELECTRICITY COSTS WATT?!

By creating a spreadsheet and graph of electricity usage and cost in an average home in their town, students will gain an understanding of the cost of electricity and how the usage fluctuates through the seasons.

Duration:

- 1 class period

Materials:

- kilowatt readings for a year (could be the teacher's readings or students' home readings)
- spreadsheet software (*Microsoft Works, ClarisWorks, AppleWorks*, etc.)

Before the computer:

- The teacher needs to obtain meter readings for his/her home for the previous year, or students need to obtain those readings by calling the electric company.
- The teacher should create a spreadsheet prior to this activity and have students enter the appropriate information.
- The spreadsheet should be saved on computers or on diskettes for student use.

On the computer:

- Use the spreadsheet to calculate monthly electrical costs based on current rate.
- Graph kilowatt/hour usage.

Option:

- Students could create this spreadsheet if they are very familiar with spreadsheet usage. They will need to be familiar with relative references and absolute references within a spreadsheet formula. Use the graph to spark a discussion of why electricity costs rise and fall according to the seasons.

	A	B	C	D	E
	Month	Starting Reading	End Reading	Difference (Kwhr)	Cost
1					
2					
3	35431	6492		=C3-B3	=0.06*D3
4	35462	=$C3		=C4-B4	=0.06*D4
5	35490	=$C4		=C5-B5	=0.06*D5
6	35521	=$C5		=C6-B6	=0.06*D6
7	35551	=$C6		=C7-B7	=0.06*D7
8	35582	=$C7		=C8-B8	=0.06*D8
9	35612	=$C8		=C9-B9	=0.06*D9
10	35643	=$C9		=C10-B10	=0.06*D10
11	35674	=$C10		=C11-B11	=0.06*D11
12	35704	=$C11		=C12-B12	=0.06*D12
13	35735	=$C12		=C13-B13	=0.06*D13
14	35765	=$C13		=C14-B14	=0.06*D14

ELECTRIC.WKS

Spreadsheet template showing formulas; months show as numerical date equivalents—the cost formula was created using $0.06 per Kwhr—check with your electric company for the current rate in your area.

ELECTRICITY COSTS WATT?! *(cont.)*

	A	B	C	D	E	F
1	Month	Starting Reading	End Reading	Difference (Kwhr)	Cost	
2						
3	January	6492	0	-6492	-389.52	
4	February	0		0		
5	March	0		0		
6	April	0		0		
7	May	0		0		
8	June	0		0		
9	July	0		0		
10	August	0		0		
11	September	0		0		
12	October	0		0		
13	November	0		0		
14	December	0		0		
15						

Spreadsheet template as students will see it (Note: Months are actual words in this view.)

	A	B	C	D	E	F
1	Month	Starting Reading	End Reading	Difference (Kwhr)	Cost	
2						
3	January	6492	7115	623	37.38	
4	February	7115	9037	1922	115.32	
5	March	9037	11752	2715	162.90	
6	April	11752	12479	727	43.62	
7	May	12479	13698	1219	73.14	
8	June	13698	15162	1464	87.84	
9	July	15162	17438	2276	136.56	
10	August	17438	19892	2454	147.24	
11	September	19892	21073	1181	70.86	
12	October	21073	22391	1318	79.08	
13	November	22391	24501	2110	126.60	
14	December	24501	26987	2486	149.16	
15						

Sample spreadsheet with end readings filled in (The spreadsheet calculated other values.)

ELECTRICITY COSTS WATT?! *(cont.)*

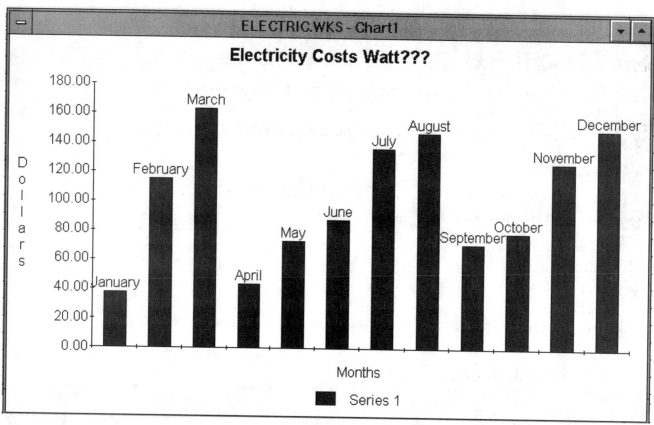

Graph of calculated electricity costs per month

Web Links:

Electricity: A Convenient Form of Energy
(brief description of electricity and how it is generated)
http://tqd.advanced.org/3501/FormsOfEnergy/Electricity/Index.html

The Electric Club
(assorted lab activities from Static Electricity to Light Emitting Diodes—LEDs)
http://schoolnet2.carleton.ca/english/math_sci/phys/electric-club/

Electricity and You
Discovery Center Science Museum
http://www.CSMATE.ColoState.EDU/DCSM/electricityampyou/

Theater of Electricity
http://www.mos.org/sln/toe/toe.html

Electricity and Electronics
http://www.rmplc.co.uk/eduWeb/sites/trinity/elec1.html

HOW DOES A COMPUTER WORK?

Students often wonder what happens inside the computer when it is turned on. These activities should satisfy their curiosity about what is inside those plastic cases.

Duration:

- This could be used as a long unit, incorporating the electronics involved, or it could be a weekly visit inside a computer.
- Five class periods would be a minimum if you have any or all of the materials.

Materials:

- a non-functional computer to take apart (several, if they are available and you have storage)
- additional non-functional computer components:

  keyboards

  hard disk drives

  floppy disk drives

  diskettes

  CD-ROM drives

  modems

  expansion cards (sound cards, video cards)

  fans

  power supplies

  motherboards

  processor chips

  computer mice or trackballs

- The Journey Inside teaching kit—available at no charge from Intel for teachers who are teaching science, math, or computers in grades five through eight
  (Contact Intel at 1-800-346-3029, ext. 143 for more information.)
- Videotape: *How Computers Work—A Journey Into the Walk-Through Computer*, The Computer Museum, Boston
- Book and CD-ROM program—*How Computers Work* or *How Multimedia Computers Work*, Ron White, PC Computing, Ziff-Davis
- Educational Activities Packet—Online Materials, The Computer Museum, Boston

Before the computer:

- Check with computer departments in high schools, colleges, and offices and with computer repair departments to find broken components they are discarding (let them know ahead of time to be on the lookout for any old components).

HOW DOES A COMPUTER WORK? *(cont.)*

Before the computer: *(cont.)*

- Access the Computer Museum Web site and print the Educational Activities Packet for integration into this unit—it is available for use whether you are able to visit the museum or not. Topics covered include the following:

    How Does a Computer Work?

    Where Did Computers Come From?

    Can Computers Think?

    How Do Computers Affect Our Lives?

    What Can You Do with a Personal Computer?

- Contact Intel for your *The Journey Inside* kit. It contains a six-unit teacher's guide, a video about what is inside a computer, a computer chip kit with silicon wafer, chips, and electronic components.

- Use *The Journey Inside* units and video to teach students about how a computer receives input, processes it, stores data, and produces output to a monitor or printer.

On the computer:

- Divide the class into teams to work through these stations:

    desktop computer parts

    Put stickers with numbers on various components and have students research to identify them.

    computer with CD-ROM or other program about how a computer works

    Depending on software available, have students use the program in order to find answers to specific questions.

    computer with online access to one of the listed sites

    Check access to these sites prior to class time and have questions set up for students to find answers for as they search through those sites.

Options:

- This unit can extend as far as you have available resources. Several have been listed, but you should contact local resources as well. Local computer stores may have employees on staff who can bring in computers and demonstrate the functions of all the components.

- If you have a network in place, have someone from your computer department take the students on a tour of the network server and cabling structure.

- Contact your local phone company about possible guest speakers who would talk to the class about cables: regular phone line, network cabling, and fiber optics.

HOW DOES A COMPUTER WORK? *(cont.)*

Web Links:

The Computer Museum—Boston
http://www.net.org/gateway/gateway.html

60 Mini-Lessons in Personal Computers
http://www.baltimorenews.com/technology/cptoc.html

Intel's Teachers Corner
http://www.intel.com/intel/educate/

Ask Doc Croc—How do computers work?
http://www.planetzoom.com/crazy/teacher/Science/Technology/adc01.html

Learn How a Computer Works Now
http://members.aol.com/amystyle/how.computers.work.html

How Computers Work—book or book & CD-ROM
Ron White—Ziff Davis Publications
available online from Amazon books
http://www.amazon.com

Indiana University School of Education
HyperTextbook: *How Computers Work*
http://education.indiana.edu/~w200/HyperTextbook/comp_wrk/topic.html

CIRCUIT—interactive tour of how a computer works (online)
Computer Interactive Resource Center Using Internet Technology
http://tqd.advanced.org/3308/

TALKING TECHIE

Your students (and you) need to learn to "talk the talk" of technology if they're going to successfully "walk the walk."

Duration:

- Spend some time each week learning new words together.

Materials:

- copies of the vocabulary list
- flashcard software (if available)
- bulletin board space to keep track of Terrific Techies (As students master this new vocabulary, award them with free computer time.)
- copies of vocabulary game software such as *WebWords*

Before the computer:

- Assign technology vocabulary words along with your regular science vocabulary lists. This should be an ongoing activity as students will be using the technology throughout the year.
- If you are using flashcard software, you will need to key in the words and definitions prior to having the students use the software.
- Make and keep regular flashcards of techie words available in the room for students to practice with when it's not their turn on the computer.

On the computer:

- Have students work in pairs or alone to practice with the technology vocabulary software. If they're in pairs, make sure they share the keyboarding task.

Option:

- Use this unit as a year-long mastery of technology vocabulary or teach it as you show the students the parts of the computer and peripheral devices and as you go online.

Web Links:

TechTools—An Informal Glossary of Introductory Internet Terms
http://curie.uncg.edu/tt/helpdesk/documents/internet/glossary.html

Digital Graphics—various educational software available
(*WebWords*—Freeware, Windows version)
http://members.aol.com/RTCCPU/Digital.htm

c|net Internet Glossary
http://www.cnet.com/Resources/Info/Glossary/index.html

StudyTech Basic Web Dictionary
http://www.studytech.com/dictionaries/basic.shtml

TALKING TECHIE *(cont.)*

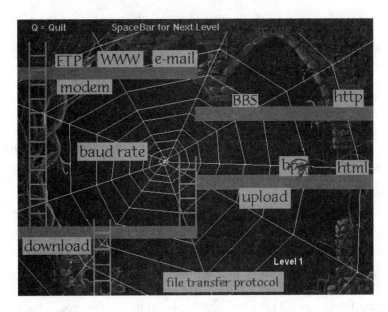

Sample screen from **WebWords**

WebWords is a freeware game for learning terms and phrases associated with the World Wide Web. The player can play any and all of the five levels or study the words and phrases in the glossary. This is a free Windows program available for download from

> Digital Graphics
> (*WebWords*—Freeware, Windows version)
> http://members.aol.com/RTCCPU/Digital.htm
> or e-mail RTCCPU@AOL.COM for more information

Mac users may want to try *Flashcard Maker*, a shareware program available for download from c|net's download site at the address below.

> *Flashcard Maker*
> c|net
> http://www.download.com

TALKING TECHIE *(cont.)*

ASCII

American Standard Code for Information Interchange—This is the computer binary code used to represent alphabetic and numerical characters using a seven-digit binary number: 0000000 through 1111111.

Bandwidth

Bandwidth is a measure of how much information you can transmit through a connection, normally measured in bits per second.

Baud

This is the rate of signal change when transmitting data.

BBS

A BBS or bulletin board system is a public place on a network that allows people to carry on discussions, upload and download files, and make announcements.

Binhex

BINary HEXadecimal is the method used for converting non-text files (non-ASCII) into ASCII code.

Bit

Short for BInary digiT, a bit is a single digit number in the binary number system, either a 1 or a 0—the smallest piece of computerized data.

Bps

Bits per second is a measurement of how fast data is moved from one place to another. A 28.8 modem can move 28,800 bits per second.

Browser

This software product is used to access and read hypertext documents on a network or on the WWW. *Netscape Navigator* is an example of a browser.

Byte

A set of eight bits that makes up a single character, a byte is the basic unit of information in a computer.

Domain Name

It is the unique name that identifies a site on the Internet.

E-mail

Electronic mail is a system for sending text messages from one person to another via computer.

TALKING TECHIE *(cont.)*

FAQ

Frequently Asked Questions—FAQs are documents or pages at Internet sites that list and answer the most commonly asked questions.

FTP

File transfer protocol is a common method of transferring files from one Internet site to another or from one computer to an Internet site.

Gigabyte

This is one billion bytes, often abbreviated to GB or G; 1000 megabytes.

Gopher

This is a menu-based system of displaying and making material available on the Internet.

Home Page

It is the Web page that your browser is set to use when it starts up or the main Web page for a business, organization, or person on the WWW.

HTML

HyperText Markup Language is the coding language used to create hypertext documents for use on the World Wide Web.

HTTP

HyperText Transport Protocol is the protocol for moving hypertext files across the Internet.

Hypertext

Hypertext is any text that contains links to other documents—words or phrases in the document are usually highlighted or underlined and can be chosen by a reader to have another screen or document appear.

Internet

This is the collection of over 60,000 inter-connected computer networks.

Intranet

This is a private network inside a company or organization.

IP Number

An Internet protocol number is a unique number consisting of four parts separated by dots such as 165.113.245.2. Every machine that is on the Internet has a unique IP number.

TALKING TECHIE *(cont.)*

ISP

An Internet service provider is a company or organization that provides access to the Internet in some form, usually for money.

Kilobyte

A kilobyte is 1024 bytes, but more frequently referred to as 1000 bytes.

LAN

A local area network is a computer network restricted to an immediate area, usually the same building or floor of a building.

List Server

This is the most common kind of e-mail mailing list. Members of a list server send mail to a central computer, and then it is sent to all members of the list.

Login

This is the account name used to gain access to a computer system or the act of entering a computer system using that name.

Megabyte

A megabyte is a million bytes, or a thousand kilobytes.

Modem

MOdulator-DEModulator—A modem is a device connected to a computer and to a phone line that allows the computer to talk to other computers through the phone system. It translates incoming analog signals into digital information for the computer and outgoing digital information into analog signals that can be carried by a standard phone line.

Network

Any time you connect two or more computers together so that they can share resources, you have a computer network.

Node

It is any single computer connected to a network.

Password

A password is a code used to gain access to a locked system.

POP

Point of presence is a location to which a network can be connected, often with dial-up phone lines.

TALKING TECHIE *(cont.)*

PPP

Point-to-point protocol is a protocol that allows a computer to use a regular telephone line and a modem to make TCP/IP connections, usually through an ISP to the Internet.

Router

A special-purpose computer (or software package), it handles the connection between two or more networks.

Server

It is a computer that provides a specific kind of service to client software running on other computers. Often, this is the computer that stores the software you access on your network.

SMTP

Simple mail transport protocol is the main protocol used to send electronic mail on the Internet.

Sysop

A SYStem OPerator is anyone responsible for the physical operations of a computer system or network resource.

TCP/IP

Transfer Control Protocol/Internet Protocol—This is the suite of protocols that defines the Internet. Often, this is the software package used to connect your computer to the Internet.

Telnet

Telnet is a program used to log in from one Internet site to another.

URL

A universal (or uniform) resource locator is the standard address of any site on the Internet that is part of the World Wide Web (WWW).

WAN

A wide area network is any network that connects an area larger than a single building.

WWW

The World Wide Web is the vast network of hypertext servers (see HTTP) which allow text, graphics, sound files, etc., to be mixed together and accessed over the Internet.

HISTORY OF COMPUTER TECHNOLOGY

We are definitely in the Technological Age. Use this lesson to take a brief look at how far we've come in the development of computers.

Duration:

- several class periods

Materials:

- reference books
- reference software and online access
- presentation software (*HyperStudio*, *The Print Shop*, HTML editor, etc.)
- time line software (*TimeLiner*)
- student work sheet, "What did I do...when...?"
- multimedia planning sheets
- colored paper for printing time lines

Optional materials:

- sticks, stones
- abacus
- sample of jacquard cloth
- punched cards
- meat skewers, rubber bands, macaroni box
- photos of the Mark I and ENIAC
- vacuum tubes (from an old radio or TV)
- photo of UNIVAC
- transistors, resistors, capacitors
- integrated circuits
- silicon chip sample
- slide set, "The History of Computers" from The Computer Museum History Center, P. O. Box 3038, Stanford, CA 94309 (415-604-2575), e-mail: allison@tcm.org
- copies of "Where Did Computers Come From" from The Computer Museum Network— Educational Activities Packet, http://www.net.org/

HISTORY OF COMPUTER TECHNOLOGY *(cont.)*

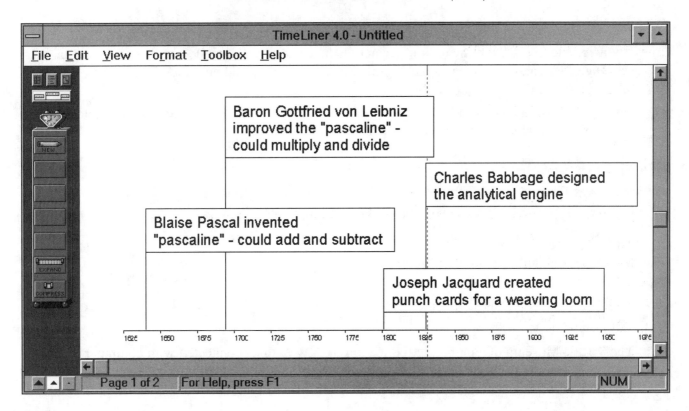

Reprinted with permission from Tom Snyder Productions, partial time line created using **Timeliner**

Before the computer:

- If you have them available, show the optional items and explain their uses.
- Give students the work sheets "What did I do...when...?" and allow time for them to find out what each of those people did.
- If reference materials are limited, make a bulletin board after a day or two with some of the elusive answers on it.
- Once students have completed the work sheets, allow them time to plan their presentations or time lines.

On the computer:

- Have students use time line software to create time lines that show the development of computer technology.
- Once they are satisfied that their time line shows all advances made, have them print it on colored paper and hang in the room or in your hallway.
- Depending on software available, have some students create multimedia presentations and later show them to the rest of the class.

HISTORY OF COMPUTER TECHNOLOGY *(cont.)*

Options:

- If you're able to get all of the optional materials listed above, you could use them as a sort of scavenger hunt and have the students figure out what they are and how they fit into the development of computer technology.

- You could make a blank time line with only the dates filled in and have the students match the developments and people to the correct dates.

Web Links:

Who Was First? A Brief Chronology of Historical Firsts in Computers (1939–1981)
http://www.apollo.co.uk/a/Lexikon/who-was-first.html

The History of Computing
http://ei.cs.vt.edu/~history/index.html

Historic Computer Images
http://ftp.arl.mil:80/ftp/historic-computers/

The Virtual Museum of Computing (collection of WWW links connected with computer history or online exhibits)
http://www.comlab.ox.ac.uk/archive/other/museums/computing.html

The History of Computing
http://irb.cs.tu-berlin.de/~zuse/history/

The Boston Computer Museum Network
http://www.net.org/

Computer History—National Museum of American History
http://www.si.edu/resource/tours/comphist/computer.htm

Slide Tour of Smithsonian Exhibit: Information Age: People, Information & Technology
http://photo2.si.edu/infoage.html

HISTORY OF COMPUTER TECHNOLOGY *(cont.)*

Brief Time Line of Computer Technology (1616–1981)

1616	John Napier, Napier's Bones
1622	William Oughtred, slide rule
1642	Blaise Pascal, Pascaline, first mechanical adding machine
1671	Gottfried von Leibnitz, first calculator
1801	Joseph Jacquard, punched cards for weaving loom
1822	Charles Babbage, analytical engine
1842	Lady Ada Augusta Lovelace, corrected errors in analytical engine
1844	Dor E. Felt, first successful adding machine (used meat skewers, rubber bands, and macaroni box)
1872	Frank S. Baldwin, first calculator invented in the U. S.
1887	Herman Hollerith, punched-card tabulating machine
1890	First automated census (using Hollerith's machine)
1903	Vacuum tube invented
1930	First analog computer
1937	Howard Aiken, Mark I
1945	Mauchly & Eckert, ENIAC
1948	Shockley, Brattain, & Bordeen, transistor invented
1951	Mauchly & Eckert, UNIVAC
1950s	Capt. Grace Hopper, applied binary number system to computers and assisted in developing COBOL (Common Business Oriented Language) programming language
1959	Integrated circuit invented
1964	John Kemeny & Thomas Kurtz, developed BASIC (Beginner's All-purpose Symbolic Instruction Code) programming language
1971	First microprocessor
1973	Altair 8800, first microcomputer
1975	Pet 2001, first single-package microcomputer
1976	Jobs & Wozniak, Apple II, first successful personal microcomputer
1981	IBM, first successfully marketed personal microcomputer

Name: _____ Date: _____

WHAT DID I DO...WHEN...?

Use reference books and/or electronic references (CD-ROM encyclopedias or online access) to find out what these people did and when they did it.

Joseph Jacquard

Dor E. Felt

Herman Hollerith

Baron Gottfried von Leibniz

William Oughtred

Howard Aiken

Charles Babbage

John Mauchly & J. P. Eckert

Lady Ada Augusta Lovelace

Capt. Grace Hopper

John Kemeny & Thomas Kurtz

John Napier

Frank S. Baldwin

Blaise Pascal

Jonathan Titus

Steve Jobs & Steve Wozniak

SHAKIN' THINGS UP

Students will use a database about earthquakes to practice sorting and querying (or searching) and answer specific questions.

Duration:

- 1 class period using the computer

Materials:

- work sheets, "Shakin' Things Up"
- earthquake database (database software—such as *Microsoft Works*, or *ClarisWorks*)

Before the computer:

- This activity should accompany lessons about plate tectonics and earthquakes and their magnitudes as measured by the Richter Scale.
- Create the earthquake database and save on lab computers or on diskettes for student access.

On the computer:

- Students should know how to use available database software.
- Have them follow the directions on the work sheet to answer questions that correlate to sorting and querying a database.

Options:

- You can continue with student interest in the data shown and have a discussion about whether magnitude is directly related to the number of deaths from an earthquake or whether the students think there might be other contributing factors.
- Have students continue the database with quakes which occurred after 1993.

Web Links:

Seismographs and the Richter Scale

    The Richter Scale
    http://www.earthsky.com/1996/es960804.html

    Measuring Earthquakes
    http://www.injersey.com/media/IonSci/graphics/earth/quakes/richter.html

    The Earthquake Pages—Richter Scale Information
    http://www.zephryus.demon.co.uk/education/geog/tectonics/earth.html

    Earthquake Magnitude Scales
    http://www.giseis.alaska.edu/Input/lahr/magnitude.html

    What Is a Seismograph?
    http://www.thetech.org/hyper/earthquakes/seismo/

SHAKIN' THINGS UP *(cont.)*

Web Links: *(cont.)*

Earthquakes

Earthquake Information from the USGS (U. S. Geological Survey)
http://quake.wr.usgs.gov/

Earthquake Information
http://www.seismo.unr.edu/htdocs/info.html

Surfing the Internet for Earthquake Data
http://www.geophys.washington.edu/seismosurfing.html

ABAG (Association of Bay Area Governments) Earthquake Maps and Information
http://www.abag.ca.gov/bayarea/eqmaps/eqmaps.html

The World-Wide Earthquake Locator (recent quakes and location map)
http://www.geo.ed.ac.uk/quakes/schools.html

Southern California Earthquake Center
http://www.usc.edu/dept/earth/quake/

Earthquake—Kobe, Japan
http://www.comet.net/earthquake/htm/kobe.htm

Tectonic Processes (list of quake resources)
http://www.cent.org/geo12/foc2b2b.htm

	DATE	YEAR	LOCATION	DEATHS	MAGNITUDE
			QUAKES.WDB		
1	August 31	1886	Charleston, SC	60	6.6
2	April 18	1906	San Francisco, CA	503	8.3
3	August 16	1906	Chile, Valparaiso	20,000	8.6
4	December 28	1908	Italy, Messina	83,000	7.5
5	January 13	1915	Italy, Avezzano	29,980	7.5
6	December 16	1920	China, Gansu	100,000	8.6
7	September 01	1923	Japan, Yokohama	200,000	8.3
8	May 22	1927	China, Nan-Shan	200,000	8.3
9	December 26	1932	China, Gansu	70,000	7.6
10	March 02	1933	Japan	2,990	8.9
11	March 10	1933	Long Beach, CA	115	6.2
12	January 15	1934	India, Bihar-Nepal	10,700	8.4

Sample view of earthquake database used in activity

Name: _____ Date: _____

SHAKIN' THINGS UP

Use the database about earthquakes to answer these questions.

Here are a few questions just to help you get familiar with the database.

1. What was the magnitude of the quake that struck Nicaragua in 1972?

2. How many quakes occurred in 1983?

3. How many deaths occurred in the quake in Southern California in 1992?

Sort the database to find the answers to the following:

4. What were the 11 strongest earthquakes? (Hint: Sort magnitude in descending order.) Fill in all the information below.

Location	Year	Magnitude	Deaths
_____	_____	_____	_____
_____	_____	_____	_____
_____	_____	_____	_____
_____	_____	_____	_____
_____	_____	_____	_____
_____	_____	_____	_____
_____	_____	_____	_____
_____	_____	_____	_____
_____	_____	_____	_____
_____	_____	_____	_____
_____	_____	_____	_____

SHAKIN' THINGS UP *(cont.)*

5. Sort the database to find out when the five least strong major earthquakes occurred.

Location   Year

_____   _____

_____   _____

_____   _____

_____   _____

_____   _____

6. Change your sort so that you find the five earthquakes with the most lives lost.

Location   Year

_____   _____

_____   _____

_____   _____

_____   _____

_____   _____

7. Query or search the database to find out how many earthquakes occurred in China.

_____

8. Query or search the database to find out how many earthquakes occurred in Turkey.

Years they occurred:

_____   _____   _____   _____

_____   _____   _____   _____

SHAKIN' THINGS UP *(cont.)*

DATABASE INFORMATION

Date	Year	Location	Deaths	Magnitude
August 31	1886	Charleston, SC	60	6.6
April 18	1906	San Francisco, CA	503	8.3
August 16	1906	Chile, Valparaiso	20,000	8.6
December 28	1908	Italy, Messina	83,000	7.5
January 13	1915	Italy, Avezzano	29,980	7.5
December 16	1920	China, Gansu	100,000	8.6
September 01	1923	Japan, Yokohama	200,000	8.3
May 22	1927	China, Nan-Shan	200,000	8.3
December 26	1932	China, Gansu	70,000	7.6
March 02	1933	Japan	2,990	8.9
March 10	1933	Long Beach, CA	115	6.2
January 15	1934	India, Bihar-Nepal	10,700	8.4
May 31	1935	India, Quetta	50,000	7.5
January 24	1939	Chile, Chillan	28,000	8.3
December 26	1939	Turkey, Erzincan	30,000	7.9
December 21	1946	Japan, Honshu	2,000	8.4
June 28	1948	Japan, Fukui	5,131	7.3
August 05	1949	Ecuador, Pelileo	6,000	6.8
August 15	1950	India, As..m	1,530	8.7
March 18	1953	NW Turkey	1,200	7.2
June 10	1956	N. Afghanistan	2,000	7.7
July 02	1957	Northern Iran	2,500	7.4
December 13	1957	Western Iran	2,000	7.1
February 01	1960	Morocco, Agadir	12,000	5.8
May 21	1960	Southern Chile	5,000	8.3
September 01	1962	Northwestern Iran	12,230	7.1
July 26	1963	Yugoslavia, Skopje	1,100	6.0
March 27	1964	Alaska	131	8.4
August 19	1966	Eastern Turkey	2,520	6.9
August 31	1968	Northeastern Iran	12,000	7.4
January 05	1970	Yunnan Province, China	10,000	7.7
March 28	1970	Western Turkey	1,086	7.4
May 31	1970	Northern Peru	66,794	7.7
February 09	1971	San Fernando Valley, CA	65	6.6
April 10	1972	Southern Iran	5,057	6.9
December 23	1972	Nicaragua	5,000	6.2
December 28	1974	Pakistan	5,200	6.3

SHAKIN' THINGS UP (cont.)

DATABASE INFORMATION (cont.)

Date	Year	Location	Deaths	Magnitude
September 06	1975	Turkey	2,312	6.8
February 04	1976	Guatemala	22,778	7.5
May 06	1976	Northeast Italy	946	6.5
June 26	1976	New Guinea, Irian Jaya	443	7.1
July 28	1976	China, Tangshan	242,000	8.2
August 17	1976	Philippines, Mindanao	8,000	7.8
November 24	1976	Eastern Turkey	4,000	7.9
March 04	1977	Romania	1,541	7.5
August 19	1977	Indonesia	200	8.0
November 23	1977	Northwestern Argentina	100	8.2
June 12	1978	Japan, Sendai	21	7.5
September 16	1978	Northeast Iran	25,000	7.7
September 12	1979	Indonesia	200	8.0
December 12	1979	Colombia, Ecuador	800	7.9
October 10	1980	Northwestern Algeria	4,500	7.3
November 23	1980	Southern Italy	4,800	7.2
December 13	1982	North Yemen	2,800	6.0
March 31	1983	Southern Colombia	250	5.5
May 26	1983	N. Honshu, Japan	81	7.7
October 30	1983	Eastern Turkey	1,300	7.1
September 19	1985	Mexico City	4,200	8.1
March 03	1985	Chile	146	7.8
March 05	1987	NE Ecuador	4,000	7.3
August 20	1988	India/Nepal border	1,000	6.5
November 06	1988	China/Burma border	1,000	7.3
December 07	1988	NW Armenia	55,000	6.8
October 17	1989	San Francisco Bay area	62	6.9
May 30	1990	Romania	8	6.5
May 30	1990	Northern Peru	115	6.3
June 21	1990	NW Iran	40,000	7.7
July 16	1990	Luzon, Philippines	1,621	7.7
February 01	1991	Pakistan/Afghanistan border	1,200	6.8
March 13	1992	Eastern Turkey	4,000	6.2
June 28	1992	Southern California	1	7.5
October 12	1992	Cairo, Egypt	450	5.9
December 12	1992	Flores, Indonesia	2,500	7.5
July 12	1993	Hokkaido, Japan	200	7.8

ROCK CYCLE

The rock cycle is the process by which rocks are created and changed by different geological processes. Students will learn about the formation of igneous, metamorphic, and sedimentary rocks through software practice and an online virtual field trip.

Duration:

- class period to teach basic steps in the rock cycle
- 1 or 2 class periods for students to solve the software rock cycle puzzle
- 1 class period for students to take the virtual field trip or for teacher to demonstrate it with overhead projector panel or PC-TV equipment

Materials:

- reference materials about rock cycle (books, reference software, online access, etc.)
- *The Rock Cycle* program by WallopWare (for Windows) available for download at most shareware sites or e-mail: wares@wallop.demon.co.uk about rockcy14.zip
- online access for virtual field trip (and additional viewing equipment for group access)
- diagrams to complete while solving software puzzle

Before the computer:

- Show students various rock samples and discuss formation of the various types of rocks (sedimentary, igneous, and metamorphic).
- Practice with the program so that you know how to exit once a student has completed it at the highest difficulty level. (Instructions are in the readme file.)

On the computer:

- Allow students time to practice with the rock cycle software program.
- It will start on the difficult level but can be changed to an easier level where it provides students with hints.
- Have students fill in the diagram as they solve the puzzle.
- Have students work in pairs or teams or use available viewing equipment for group viewing to visit the virtual field trip at Texas A&M's Big Bend National Park Virtual Field Trip. http://geoWeb.tamu.edu/faculty/herbert/bigbend/

Option:

- Have students create multimedia presentations using software such as *HyperStudio* or HTML coding to illustrate the rock cycle, incorporating digital images of rocks you have available or they have collected.

ROCK CYCLE *(cont.)*

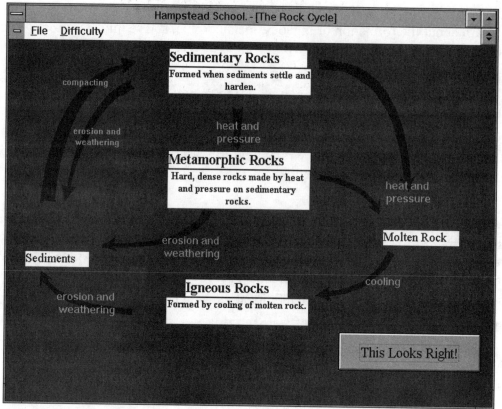

Screen shot of The Rock Cycle program with correct solution

Web Links:

Shareware.Com
search for rock cycle software for downloading freeware program
http://www.shareware.com

Science Web—The Burgess Shale Project—Geology—Origin & Format
http://scienceWeb.dao.nrc.ca/burgess/geology/cycle1.html

The Rock Cycle
http://duke.usask.ca/~reeves/prog/geoe118/geoe118.011.html

Anglia Education—The Rock Cycle
http://www.anglia.co.uk/angmulti/learning/science/chem4/rock/cycle.html

VolcanoWorld—Rock Cycle
http://volcano.und.nodak.edu/vwdocs/vwlessons/lessons/Rocks/Rocks6.html

University of British Columbia—Petrology—Rock Cycle
http://www.science.ubc.ca/~geol202/rock_cycle/rockcycle.html

All You Ever Need to Know About Rock Cycles
http://science.coe.uwf.edu/SH/Curr/rockcyc/rockcyc.htm

Name: _____   Date:

STUDY DIAGRAM

Fill in the appropriate rock types and formation descriptions as found in the program *The Rock Cycle*. Draw arrows where they belong and in the correct directions. Label the arrows to match the rock cycle.

Rocks
_____
Formation:

Rocks
_____
Formation:

Rocks
_____
Formation:

ROCKHOUNDS

Rockhounds may actually be "mineral hounds"—collecting specimens of minerals and gemstones. Most collectors save every kind of mineral they find, but specialized collectors only collect specimens which belong to certain groups of minerals. In either case, organization by group is an important process. This database activity and assorted references will help you and your students identify and maintain organized collections.

Duration:

- several class periods

Materials:

- rock, mineral, gem specimens
- field guides and other reference books
- hand lens
- streak plates (or ceramic tiles—from hardware store—You may be able to obtain broken tiles for free and simply tape the sharp edges.)
- copper penny
- table knife
- plate glass
- steel file
- database software
- mineral identification and database software

    The Mineral Database, LR Ream Publishing, http://www.iea.com/~lream/

    Learn by Doing—Science Labs—kits with accompanying CD-ROM (minerals, rocks, fossils) http://www.swiftsite.com/ScienceLabs/

Before the computer:

- Collect or purchase rock, mineral, and gem specimens (from science supply stores, catalogs, or online resources).
- Show example specimens or photos of the different physical properties of minerals.
- Have students bring in rock and mineral specimens. (Make marks on the bottoms of their specimens with white correction fluid and then write their initials on the white space with a felt-tip marker.)
- Have students bring in egg cartons (or plastic specimen boxes if they prefer) to organize their collections.
- Students will use reference books and field guides, as well as software or online references, to identify their specimens.

ROCKHOUNDS *(cont.)*

Before the computer: *(cont.)*

- Students will complete testing of physical properties:

Color

under normal light, ultraviolet light, when wet or dry

Streak

color when scratched across a streak plate or the unglazed underside of a porcelain tile

Hardness

assorted hardness scales—Moh's scale is widely used.

Transparency

how a mineral lets light pass through it—transparent, translucent, or opaque

Luster

metallic, submetallic, vitreous or glassy, adamantine or diamondlike, resinous, silky, pearly, greasy or oily, waxy, or earthy

Cleavage

the break in a crystal face where a new crystal is forming

Fracture

a place where the mineral is chipped

On the computer:

- Use a software database such as *The Mineral Database* to match the results of properties testing to the correct minerals.

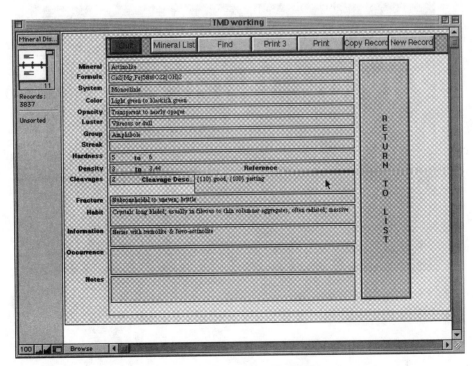

Sample screen from **The Mineral Database***, L. R. Ream Publishing*

ROCKHOUNDS (cont.)

On the computer: (*cont.*)

- Have students enter their data into a simple database (sample shown here can be extended, depending on your testing capabilities).

	Mineral	Color	Streak	Hardness	Transparency	Luster	Cleavage	Fracture	
1									
2									
3									
4									
5									
6									
7									

Data2

Sample database screen for organizing mineral collection

- If there are enough specimens, you should also organize them according to classes of minerals:

elements	sulfates
sulfides	phosphates
halides	silicates
oxides	organic minerals
carbonates	

- Have students use specimen identification programs, such as *Rock Lab* or *Mineral Lab*, to lead them through the testing of rocks and minerals and identifying them.

Learn by Doing *CD-ROM programs and specimen kit*

ROCKHOUNDS *(cont.)*

*Information Screens from **Rock Lab***

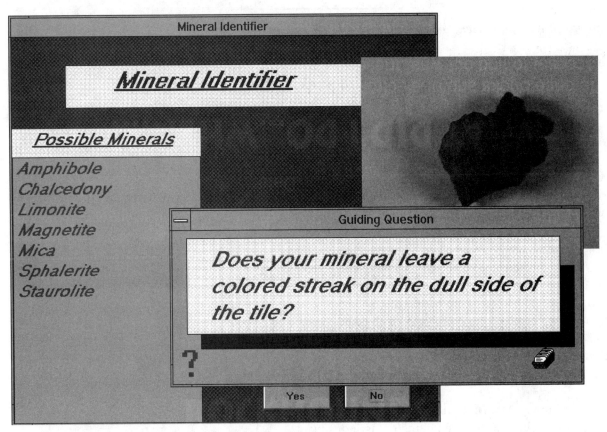

*Identification screens from **Mineral Lab***

ROCKHOUNDS *(cont.)*

Options:

- Have students photograph their specimens with a digital camera (even one as simple as a black and white QuickCam from Connectix) just to have a reference as to which mineral specimen is being identified and include the photo with their database information.

- Have students create multimedia presentations of their rock/mineral collections, using data about physical properties and photos taken with digital cameras. They could either use their own collections or use this as a project to catalog your classroom specimens. Add to that presentation each year as you add specimens to the collection.

- Stretch this project if you are in a larger school with more than one set of mineral specimens. Create multimedia presentations with the data and photographs of specimens in all classrooms in your school. Then share the software with all classrooms if the specimens can't be transferred from room to room.

Sample photo of rock specimen, taken with a black & white QuickCam

Web Links:

The Mineral & Gemstone Kingdom
http://www.minerals.net

Rockhounds Information Page
http://www.rahul.net/infodyn/rockhounds/rockhounds.html

Bob's Rock Shop
http://www.rockhounds.com

Moh's Scale
http://www.museum.state.il.us/isas/kingdom/geo1003.html

Gem Explorer: Moh's Scale of Hardness
http://www.gemexplorer.com/moh.html

Minerals
http://www.geo.utep.edu:80/epgeofaqs/minerals/Definition.html

Smithsonian Gem & Mineral Collection
http://galaxy.einet.net/images/gems/gems-icons.html

ROCKHOUNDS *(cont.)*

Web Links: *(cont.)*

CataLynx Geology Page
http://www.intrepid.net/~hollyoak/geology.htm

Earth Science *HyperStudio* Stacks (for the Mac)
http://volcano.und.nodak.edu/downloads/stack.html

RING OF FIRE

Rather than building models of volcanoes that erupt with baking soda and vinegar, have your students identify the location of the Ring of Fire by researching volcano locations around the world.

Duration:

- several class periods, depending on depth of research

Materials:

- *World Almanac* (for list of Notable Active Volcanoes)
- reference materials (books, electronic encyclopedias, online access)
- large paper world map—suitable for pinning (hang on a bulletin board)
- map pins or small pins with flags
- Download the demo *Magic Schoolbus Explores Inside the Earth—Volcanoes* and install it on your computer.

Before the computer:

- Assign each student a volcano to research.
- Have students use library resources, electronic encyclopedias, and other software or online access to research their volcano.
- Once they locate the volcano, have them mark it on a world map with a pin or tiny flag.

On the computer:

- Students will research their assigned volcano by using library resources, electronic reference materials, or online access.
- They will then mark their volcano's location on the world map in the classroom.
- Students can use volcano simulation to learn about the different types of volcanic formations and eruptions.

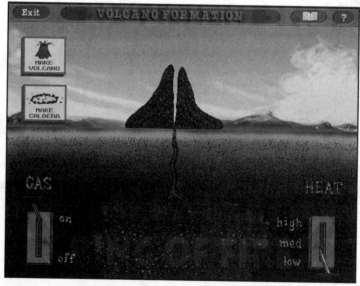

Screen from demo **The Magic School Bus—Volcanoes**

RING OF FIRE *(cont.)*

Options:

- This lesson can be extended into a group multimedia program. Each student could create a *HyperStudio* card to be included in one large stack compiling all the researched volcanoes.
- Students can create a database of volcanoes. Database could include name, location, and date of last activity.
- Instead of having each student research one volcano, you can have the students research the locations of 10–15 of the volcanoes on the list and then plot them on a world map. This should lead students into visualizing the Ring of Fire.

Web Links:

Ring of Fire: This Dynamic Earth (USGS)
http://pubs.usgs.gov/publications/text/fire.html

Volcano World
http://volcano.und.nodak.edu/

Volcanoes and Earthquakes
http://pibWeb.it.nwu.edu/~pib/volcanos.htm

Michigan Technological University Volcanoes Page
http://www.geo.mtu.edu/volcanoes/

The Volcanic Jump Station
http://www.aist.go.jp/GSJ/~jdehn/vjump.htm

Ken Wright's Volcano Home Page
http://www.southern.edu:80/people/kawright/homepage/m.htm

The Electronic Volcano
http://www.dartmouth.edu/~volcano/

Welcome to Volcano Alive (a student activity)
http://www.4j.lane.edu/Personal/C/Carper/Project/Project.html

Magic School Bus Explores Earth–Volcano Builder (free preview from Microsoft, Inc.)
Change the gas and temperature settings to create a volcano.
available for free download at ZDNet Software Library
http://www.hotfiles.com/

Microsoft Teacher Activity Guides
http://www.microsoft.com/education/curric/

RING OF FIRE *(cont.)*

ACTIVE VOLCANOES AS OF MAY 1996

Acatenango	Fuego	Makushin	Sakura-jima
Akita	Komaga-take Fuji	Manam	San Cristobal
Akutan	Galaggung	Masaya	San Miguel
Alaid	Galeras	Mauna Loa	Sangay
Ambrym	Gamalama	Mayon	Sangeeang Api
Arenal	Gamkonora	Merapi	Santa Maria
Asama	Gareloi	Momotombo	Santorini
Aso	Great Sitkin	Nasu	Sarychev Peak
Augustine	Guagua Pichincha	Ngauruhoe	Seguam
Awu	Guallatiri	Niigata Yake-yama	Semeeru
Azuma	Hekia	Novarupta	Shasta
Baganaa	Iliamna	Nyamuragira	Shishaldin
Baitoushan	Irazú	Nyiragogo	Siamet
Bandai	Karangetang	Okmok	Soputan
Beerenberg	Karkar	Ol Doinyo Lengai	Soufrière St. Vincent
Bezymianny	Karthala	On-take	St. Helens
Bulusan	Karymsky	Oshima	Stromboli
Cameroon	Kelud	Póas	Suwanose-jima
Canlaon	Kerinci	Pacaya	Taal
Cerro Hudson	Kilauea	Pagan	Tacana
Chokai	Kirishima	Pavlof	Tiatia
Citlaltepeti	Kiska	Pelee	Tolbachik
Cleveland	Kliuchevskoi	Pinatubo	Tupungatito
Colima	Korovin	Piton de la Fournaise	Turrialba
Concepción	Krafla	Popocatépetl	Ulawun
Cotpaxi	Krakatau	Purace	Unzen
Deception Island	Láscar	Rabaul	Usu
El Chichon	Lake Nyos	Rainier	Veniaminof
El Misti	Langila	Raung	Villarrica
Erta-Alw	Llaima	Redoubt	White Island
Erubus	Llullaillaco	Rincón de la Vieja	Wrangell
Etna	Lokon-Empung	Ruapehu	
Fernandina	Lopevi	Ruiz	

RING OF FIRE *(cont.)*

WORLD MAP

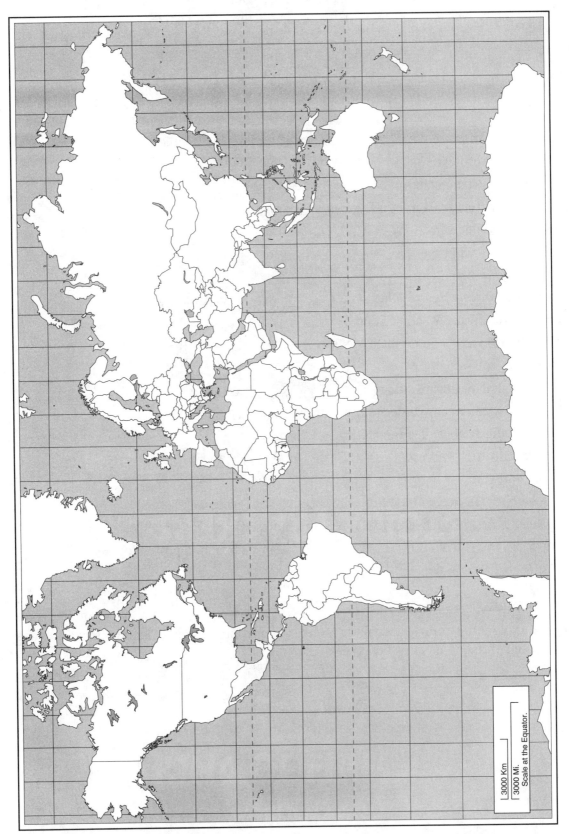

3000 Km
3000 Mi.
Scale at the Equator.

WEATHER DATA

Weather can be studied year-round, and what better way to collect data than to use your computer? Students can fill in the database, compare/contrast their data with professionally collected data, and view weather trends over months and years by having their data organized.

Duration:

- short portion of each class period throughout the year (for best comparisons)

Materials:

- manual weather data collection tools (as many of these as possible):
    barometer (air pressure)
    thermometer (temperature)
    hygrometer (relative humidity)
    wind vane (wind direction)
    anemometer (wind speed)
    rain gauge (precipitation)
- electronic/computerized weather station equipment (if available):
    AWS—Automated Weather Source
    AWS Worldwide School Weather Network
    http://www.aws.com
    AWE Digital Weather Station
    http://www.americanweather.com/wps.html
- weekly weather data collection sheets
- database software (*Microsoft Works*, *ClarisWorks*, *AppleWorks*, etc.)
- weather software:
    WinWeather (Insanely Great Software, http://www.igsnet.com/)
    Weather Tracker (KIDware, 15600 NE 8th, Suite B1-314, Bellevue, WA 98008)
    (other programs that allow you to access weather data from a professional source)
- online access (Many sites online report current data.)

Before the computer:

- Collect weather data using manual instruments and record that data on a daily chart. (That job could rotate through the class on a weekly basis.)

WEATHER DATA *(cont.)*

On the computer:

- Gather professional data by using *WinWeather* set to your closest city or by using online resources.

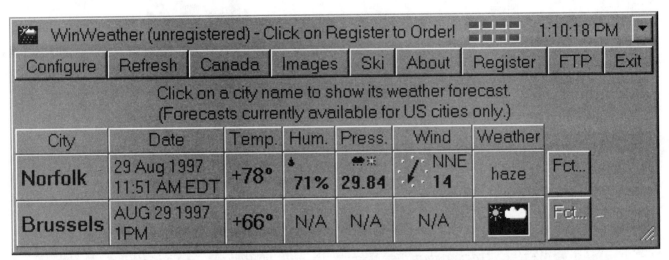

*Screen print from **WinWeather** showing available data for Norfolk, VA, and Brussels, Belgium*

- Compare/contrast daily collections. (Discuss whether differences are due to distance between locations or to instrument fallibility or to human fallibility or error.)
- Study weather trends as they compare with previous year's data. (Keep data from year to year and use software such as *Weather Tracker* or your database program to graph comparisons of certain fields of data.)

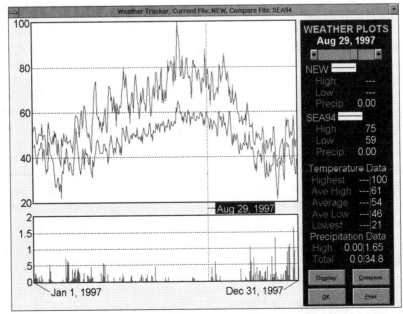

*Screen print of **Weather Tracker** showing weekly precipitation plotted for the year 1994—This program compares current collected data with previous years' stored data.*

WEATHER DATA *(cont.)*

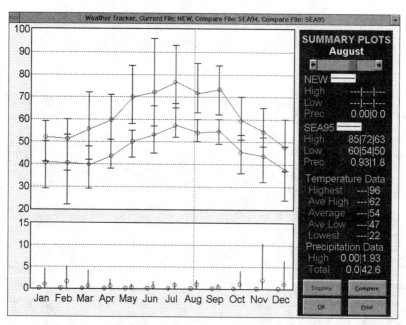

Screen print from **Weather Tracker** *showing temperature data plotted for the year 1995*

	Date	Time	Bar. Press.	Temp.	Rel. Humid.	Wind Dir.	Wind Speed	Precip.	Weather Cond.
1									
2									
3									
4									
5									
6									

WEATHER.WDB

Sample database for organizing weather data

Options:

- Look at some of the activities online at "Weather Here and There." It is an integrated weather unit incorporating hands-on, collaborative, problem-solving activities with the Internet. The activities are geared for students in grades four through six.

- Some TV stations have weather programs where they allow schools and individuals to submit weather (particularly rain) data to the station. One such station is WTOC 11 in Savannah, Georgia. You might want to check with your local station to see if they accept such data or offer interactive programs.

- If you are studying other specific regions or states (or even other countries), you can check their weather data through online newspaper or TV or radio station listings. A super collection of those Web links can be found at Newspaper Mania. Multilingual students can also read and report the weather from papers written in other languages.

WEATHER DATA *(cont.)*

Web Links:

National Weather Service—Interactive Weather Information Network (IWIN)
http://140.90.6.254/

EarthWatch Communications, Inc.
3-D weather information and forecasts
http://www.earthwatch.com/index.html

Weather Wise Education Modules
http://oldthunder.ssec.wisc.edu/wxwise/madstat.html

SuperNet Education Channel—Weather Education
http://www.itl.net/Education/online/weather/

Weather Education Page
http://nimbo.wrh.noaa.gov/Portland/educate.html

Weather Here and There
http://www.ncsa.uiuc.edu/edu/RSE/RSEred/WeatherHome.html

The Weather Channel—Learn More
http://www.weather.com/learn_more/

WeatherNet
live cameras in cities around North America, weather software, data, etc.
http://cirrus.sprl.umich.edu/wxnet/

Interactive Weather Information Network
http://140.90.6.254/

Vortex Consulting—Meteorology Wizard
conversion program for Win'95—calculates heat index, wind chill, etc.
http://www.cybercomm.net/~tornado/metwiz.html

WTOC-TV 11 Savannah, GA
http://www.wtoctv.com/weather/joinwt.htm

Newspaper Mania—Internet Press North America
newspapers from all states and Canadian provinces—with local weather listings
fantastic resource for finding specific daily information
http://www.club.innet.be/~year0230/american.htm

Name: _____   Date: _____

WEEKLY WEATHER DATA COLLECTION FORM

Week of _____ to _____

Date	_____	_____	_____	_____	_____
Time	_____	_____	_____	_____	_____
Barometric Pressure	_____	_____	_____	_____	_____
Temperature	_____	_____	_____	_____	_____
Relative Humidity	_____	_____	_____	_____	_____
Wind Direction	_____	_____	_____	_____	_____
Wind Speed	_____	_____	_____	_____	_____
Precipitation	_____	_____	_____	_____	_____
Cloud Cover	_____	_____	_____	_____	_____
General Weather Conditions	_____	_____	_____	_____	_____

STORM TRACKERS

Hurricane tracking can allow students to practice their latitude and longitude plotting skills while learning about air currents and warm and cold water currents. Those students near the coastlines will also have a better understanding of what a hurricane is doing if they are able to plot and follow it on paper or on a computer program.

Duration:

- short time period of several class periods (depending on duration of the storm)

Materials:

- access to weather data by way of radio, television, or online access
- hurricane tracking charts and software

Before the computer:

- Students should have ample practice plotting coordinates on sample tracking charts. (Both Atlantic and Pacific coast charts are available online.)
- Listen to daily or hourly updates on positions of current hurricanes.

On the computer:

- Have students plot the coordinates of past or current hurricanes on tracking software.
- Once they finish data input, they can watch the animation of the hurricane travel along its track.
- Storm data can be saved and recalled later to compare/contrast several storms.
- Historical data is also available for notable storms of the past.

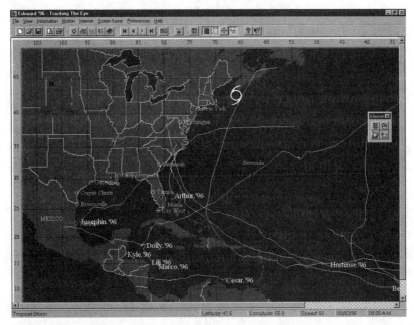

*Screen shot from **Tracking the Eye** by Gencode, http://www.gencode.com/hurricane/hurricane.htm*

STORM TRACKERS *(cont.)*

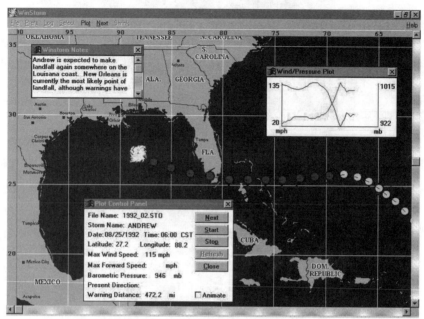

*Screen shot from **WinStorm** by Ingramation, http://www.ghgcorp.com/kingram/index.html*

Options:

- If you do not live near a hurricane area, try plotting past hurricanes or inland storm tracks.

Web Links:

National Hurricane Center/Tropical Prediction Center
http://www.nhc.noaa.gov/index.html

The Weather Page: Storm Center (hurricane information)
http://www.umassd.edu/Menus/stormcenter.html

The Wrath of Nature (storm images and additional Web links)
http://pw1.netcom.com/~jmlcat-5/index.html

Tropical Oceans—Tropical Cyclones (tracking graphics and charts online)
http://lumahai.soest.hawaii.edu/Tropical_Weather/

Hurricanes, Typhoons & Tropical Cyclones
http://www.solar.ifa.hawaii.edu/Tropical/tropical.html

Hurricane Resource Center
http://www.jones.edu/JCHC/

THE UNIVERSE

Comets, stars, planets, galaxies.... students can find them all with the help of some great simulation programs. Students can also use resources and information to identify objects in their own night skies and to create multimedia projects.

Duration:

- several class periods

Materials:

- reference materials (books, electronic encyclopedias, online access)
- sign-making/presentation/multimedia software (*The Print Shop*, *HyperStudio*, etc.)
- multimedia planning sheets

Before the computer:

- Download and install software for student use.
- Have students do basic research in books, periodicals, etc., in your media center.
- Assign or have students choose an astronomy topic of interest to create their multimedia presentation.

On the computer:

- Have students find additional data about their subject in electronic reference materials or online.
- There are also many sources of graphics and animations online for educational use. (Students can learn to download them and use them in their multimedia presentations.)
- Students will develop a multimedia presentation to illustrate their topic.

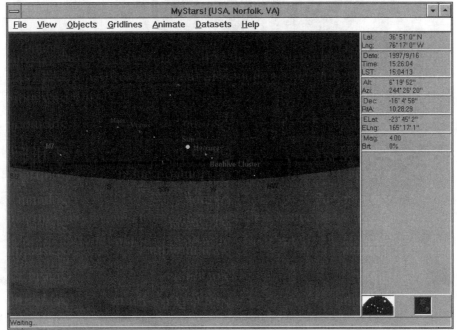

*The program **MyStars!** can be set to coordinates near your location and will show an animation of the night sky.*

THE UNIVERSE *(cont.)*

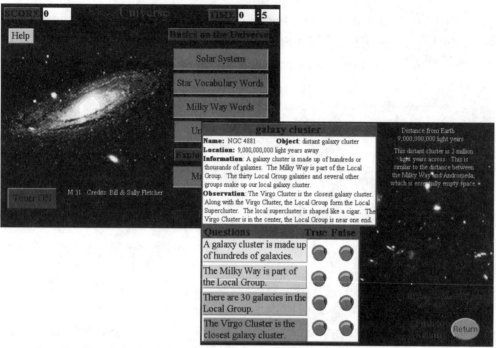

Jackson and Tull's **Exploring the Universe** *teaches students through the use of a quiz-type program. (Several other free programs are also available.)*

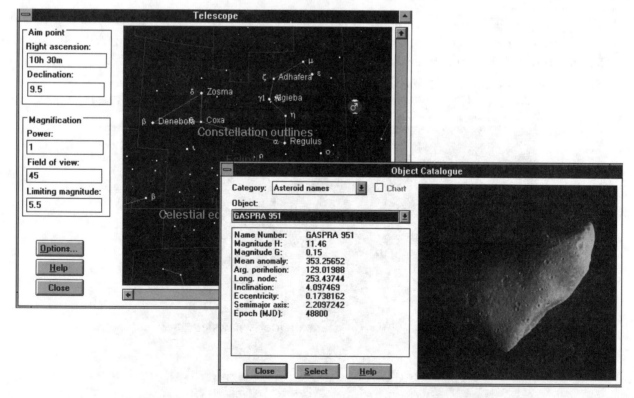

Home Planet, *another free software program, includes an Earth map, Sun and Moon position data, sky map, and a database of over 5000 asteroids and comets.*

THE UNIVERSE *(cont.)*

Options:

- You could assign this as a group project by dividing your classroom into teams and assigning each team a particular topic such as comets, galaxies, planets, moons, or stars.
- Use Tom Snyder Productions' *The Great Solar System Rescue* to integrate history, astronomy, meteorology, and geology as students work as collaborating scientists.

Web Links:

NASA Spacelink—An Aeronautics and Space Resource for Educators
http://spacelink.nasa.gov/.index.html

The Adler Planetarium and Astronomy Museum
Connecting to the Universe
http://www.adler.uchicago.edu/universe/Universe.htm

Jackson and Tull's PCs IN SPACE
http://hst-nic.hst.nasa.gov/space/index2.html

PlanetWatch
http://www.raben.com/planet/Plnwch.html

Night Sky
http://www.beachware.com/NightSky.html

Relative Data Products—MyStars!
http://www.relativedata.com/mystars/

The Astronomy Slide Show—free software
http://home.inreach.com/jayrob/

Home Planet—free software
http://www.fourmilab.ch/homeplanet/homeplanet.html

Hubble Space Telescope's Greatest Hits 1990–1995 Gallery
http://oposite.stsci.edu/pubinfo/BestOfHST95.html

Astronomical Pictures & Animations
http://www.univ-rennes1.fr/ASTRO/astro.english.html

Universe in the Classroom—free print or online quarterly newsletter
http://www.aspsky.org/subpages/tnl1.html

Mike Boschat's Astronomy Page (a resource list of astronomy links online)
http://www.atm.dal.ca/~andromed/

MULTIMEDIA PLANNING SHEET

Title Card

Buttons/Links: _____

Notes (Text/Sounds/Animations): _____

Card 1

Buttons/Links: _____

Notes (Text/Sounds/Animations): _____

Card 2

Buttons/Links: _____

Notes (Text/Sounds/Animations): _____

Card 3

Buttons/Links: _____

Notes (Text/Sounds/Animations): _____

Card 4

Buttons/Links: _____

Notes (Text/Sounds/Animations): _____

Card 5

Buttons/Links: _____

Notes (Text/Sounds/Animations): _____

HOW CURRENT IS THE DATA?

With the Hubble telescope and the Pathfinder mission revealing more information about our universe, students need to realize that reference materials from even a few years ago may not have current data in them. This activity will help them learn to check the reliability of the source of information for all research projects.

Duration:

- 2 class periods (1 for researching library texts and 1 for computer software or online work)

Materials:

- reference books about planets (Ask to borrow all of the planet reference materials for the day.)
- reference software programs (planets, solar system, encyclopedias)
- online access (Visit the Web sites listed.)

Before the computer:

- Have the students work in teams or pairs to find data about the planets from reference books (either in your room or in the library/media center).

On the computer:

- Have the students find the same pieces of data from a current software program or online.

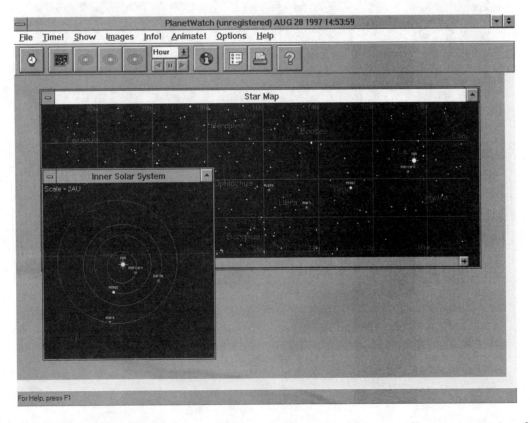

PlanetWatch *by Galen Raben has animated views of planets in orbit as well as an extensive database of information about each planet.*

HOW CURRENT IS THE DATA? *(cont.)*

On the computer: *(cont.)*

- Have class discussion about the "age" of the data they retrieved from the books vs. the "age" of the data from the software programs and online sources.

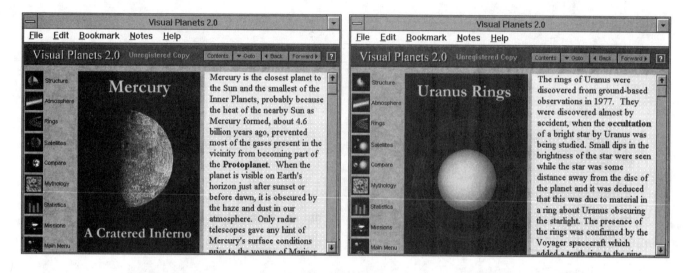

*Samples of types of data found about individual planets in Pulsar Publishing's **Visual Planets***

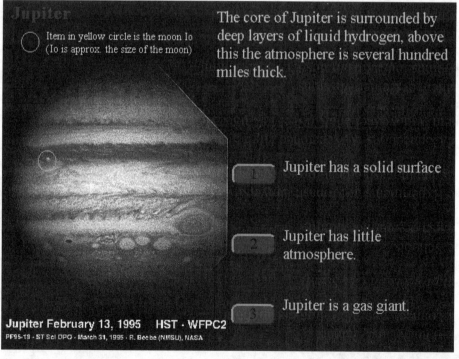

*Jackson and Tull's free **Solar System** software lets students follow a quiz format to learn about the planets.*

HOW CURRENT IS THE DATA? *(cont.)*

Options:

- Students can organize their data by creating a small database for all reference material used.
- Have students copy their chart onto large chart paper to hang in the room and share with the entire class.

	Planet	Diameter (km)	Dist. from Sun	Rotation (hrs)	Revolution(yrs)	Rings	Moons
1	Mercury						
2	Venus						
3	Earth						
4	Mars						
5	Jupiter						
6	Saturn						
7	Uranus						
8	Neptune						
9	Pluto						

PLANETS.WDB

Sample planets database screen

Web Links:

NASA Spacelink—An Aeronautics & Space Resource for Educators
http://spacelink.nasa.gov/.index.html

The Nine Planets
http://seds.lpl.arizona.edu/nineplanets/nineplanets/

Welcome to the Planets
http://pds.jpl.nasa.gov/planets/

Mars Pathfinder Mission
http://www.jpl.nasa.gov/mpfmir/

Jackson and Tull's PCs IN SPACE
http://hst-nic.hst.nasa.gov/space/index2.html

Pulsar Publishing—Visual Planets
http://www.astrosoftware.com/

PlanetWatch
http://www.raben.com/planet/Plnwch.html

Name: _____   Date: _____

HOW CURRENT IS THE DATA?

Find the following information in two different reference materials. The first should be a book, and the second should be an electronic reference source (CD-ROM or an online source).

Reference source #1:_____   **Copyright date:**_____

	Mercury	Venus	Earth	Mars	Jupiter	Saturn	Uranus	Neptune	Pluto
Diameter (km)									
Distance from sun									
Rotation period (hrs)									
Revolution period (years)									
Rings									
Moons (satellites)									

Reference source #2:_____   **Copyright date:**_____

	Mercury	Venus	Earth	Mars	Jupiter	Saturn	Uranus	Neptune	Pluto
Diameter (km)									
Distance from sun									
Rotation period (hrs)									
Revolution period (years)									
Rings									
Moons (satellites)									

NASA-TV ON CU-SEEME

NASA Television provides the American people access through television to their aeronautics and space program. These broadcasts are available via *CU-SeeMe* technology through your Internet connection.

Duration:

- 1 class period for paper activity simulation flip book of robot arm manipulations
- many class periods or portions to observe future shuttle and rocket launches and missions

Materials:

- online access
- *CU-SeeMe* software (from Cornell or White Pine)
- copies of flip book simulation work sheet

Before the computer:

- Have students cut the pictures from the simulation work sheet, stack them, and then staple them at the top to form a flip book.
- Let them flip the pages to observe how they will view something on *CU-SeeMe*. (The transmissions are not always fluid in motion but are more like pictures flipping past.)
- Download and install *CU-SeeMe* software so that you will be able to observe NASA missions.
- Check the NASA schedule (posted on the NASA-TV Web site) to find an activity during your class times.

On the computer:

- Connect to a NASA-TV reflector site via your *CU-SeeMe* software. (Several addresses are listed on the NASA-TV Web site.)
- Have students observe launches, mission activities, interviews with astronauts, mission control operations, and transmissions of past observations from space.

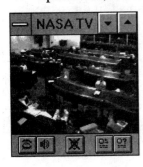   

1.   2.   3.   4.

Views from Space Shuttle Discovery's mission STS-85 in August 1997
1. Mission Control in Houston, Texas; 2. robot arm manipulation with Earth in background; 3. Canadian astronaut Bjarni Tyggvason during an interview with Canadian students; 4. view of the sun setting over the horizon of the Earth as the shuttle continues its orbit

NASA-TV ON CU-SEEME *(cont.)*

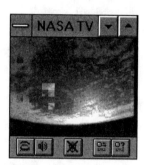

CU-SeeMe
Screen size 160 x 120

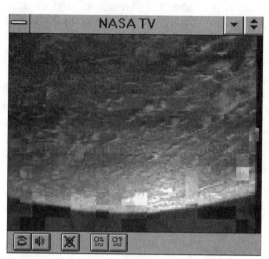

CU-SeeMe
Screen size 320 x 240

Views from NASA archives of pictures of Earth from orbiting satellites and space shuttles

Options:

- If events are appearing at times other than your scheduled class time, you can videotape your computer screen while utilizing a computer-to-TV connection. Many of those devices, particularly the PC-to-TV connections by AITech, connect through your VCR before connecting to the television. You can also double your viewing ability by connecting your computer to the television (or to more than one television by using a signal splitter) as your class watches transmissions.

- Use your *CU-SeeMe* software with a computer video camera, such as the QuickCam by Connectix, to connect with other students around the world. You can connect directly to another computer for one-to-one conversations. To allow more than one school to connect to the same conversation, you would need to access a reflector (CU computer server) site. Some sites online will allow you to use their reflector space and time for educational activities if you contact them and schedule that use ahead of time. Some educational reflector sites, such as the Global Schoolhouse and the Challenger Learning Center, schedule activities for various classes to join.

- To get in touch with schools around the world using *CU-SeeMe* video conferencing software, subscribe to the CU-SeeMe-Schools list server by sending an e-mail to lists@gsn.org. The body of the e-mail should contain only the following information: subscribe cuseeme-schools Your Name.

NASA-TV ON CU-SEEME *(cont.)*

Web Links:

NASA-TV Links

NASA-TV Web site
http://btree.lerc.nasa.gov/NASA_TV/NASA_TV.html

STS-85 Page (for further information about the mission used in this lesson)
http://shuttle.nasa.gov/sts-85/

CU-SeeMe Technology Links

Cornell University's CU-SeeMe Page
http://cu-seeme.cornell.edu/

White Pine CU-SeeMe Software
http://www.cu-seeme.com

Connectix—QuickTime Camera
http://www.connectix.com/html/quickcam.html

Schools and joint projects on CU-SeeMe

CU-SeeMe Schools
http://www.gsn.org/cu/index.html

CU-SeeMe Experiments at Monash University
http://edx1.educ.monash.edu.au/projects/cuseeme/

CU-SeeMe Connections at Wenatchee High School
http://einstein.wsd.wednet.edu/CuSeeMe/CuSeeMe.html

Online Challenger Center Missions
http://www.hmns.mus.tx.us./hmns/CU-SeeMe.html

Challenger Learning Center
http://www.hmns.mus.tx.us/hmns/challenger.html

"Public Connection" Project
Earth views of space and space views of Earth
http://space.rice.edu/hmns/

Sharing NASA
(interactive projects between students and working professionals)
http://quest.arc.nasa.gov/interactive/

NASA-TV ON CU-SEEME *(cont.)*

The Space Shuttle Discovery mission STS-85, launched on August 7, 1997, lasted for 13 days before they landed on August 19. During the mission, one of the tasks was to demonstrate Japan's newly designed dexterous robot arm in the space environment before installing it on the Japanese Experiment Module (JEM) of the International Space Station.

Carefully cut out each of these photographs and then staple them together at the top. Hold the top of the stack (book) and flip with the fingers of your other hand to observe how you would view this on *CU-SeeMe* as the robot arm opens and then closes a compartment door.

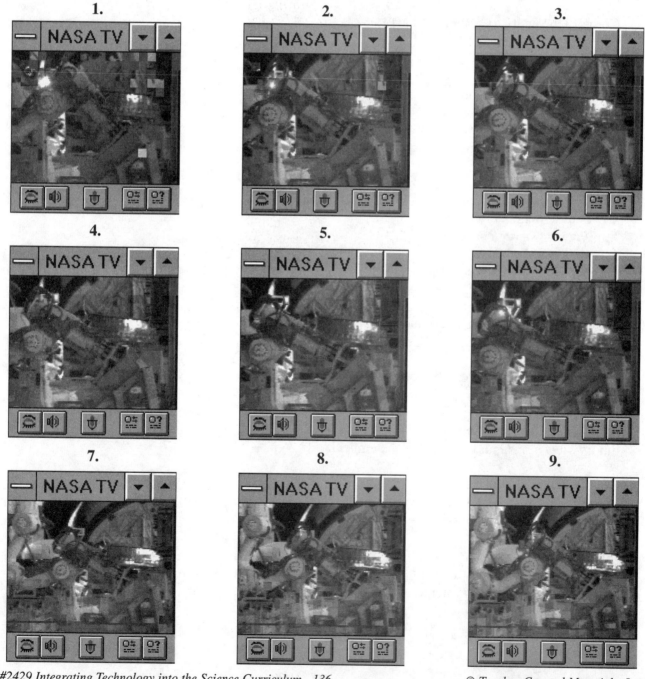

NASA-TV ON CU-SEEME *(cont.)*

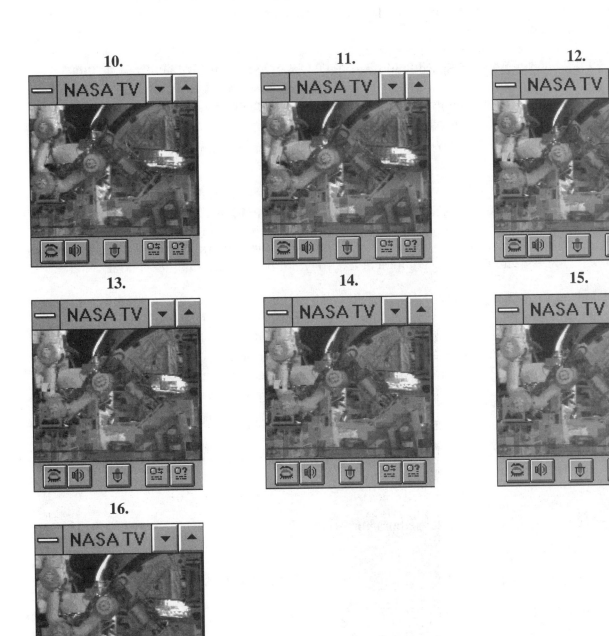

SCIENCE PROJECTS

Science projects can often be the bane of a science teacher's (or parent's) existence. If not monitored closely, they can quickly become a weekend activity which is stressful for both the student and the parents. Try something different by requiring your students to use as much of your available technology as possible.

- Use multimedia software (*HyperStudio* or a Web browser to create presentations to accompany their projects.
- Create time lines to show the progression of some aspect of their experiment, particularly if it is one requiring a lengthy observation time.
- Set up spreadsheets from collected numerical data and use the graphing or charting feature of the software package to make professional quality graphs.
- Organize survey data in a database and include that on the display or in the report.
- Utilize still or video digital images in displays, reports, and multimedia presentations.

Simply make sure that your students are aware of all the possibilities. Work with media coordinators in other schools in your system to borrow equipment that may not be in use at another school.

Publish a record of your class' projects. Whether you take digital photographs of students and projects at the fair or collect photos as students are working on their projects during school time, utilize the technology yourself. Make a scrapbook by integrating those digital images into word-processed pages or create a multimedia project to show at next year's open house or develop a Web site and post those pictures online for all school parents to view. If students know ahead of time that their work will be published, they may put a little more effort into making it a better project.

Web Links:

Experimental Science Projects: An Introductory Level Guide
http://www.isd77.k12.mn.us/resources/cf/SciProjIntro.html

Science Fairs and Science Projects
http://www.gallaudet.edu/~mssdsci/scifairs.html

Multimedia Science Projects
http://www.educ.ksu.edu/Projects/JRCE/v28-5/mcgrath/article/main.htm

Science Projects (list of Web links)
http://www.ecesc.k12.in.us/projects.html

SCIENCE REPORTS

If you are requiring your students to use a word processer for their reports, here are a few guidelines for you (and them).

- Start with a basic outline.
- Thoroughly research the concepts on the outline.
- Key in the content of the paper using a simple font. (Don't waste computer time choosing a pretty font. This is a science report, not a friendly letter.)
- Use the spell-check feature of the word processor.
- Switch places with someone else and proofread each other's papers.
- Print a first draft in "draft mode." This conserves ink while printing a hard copy that the student can then take home and edit.
- Practice editing marks while self-editing this draft.
- Spend another day editing the report at the computer.
- Make sure the title page follows specific guidelines. Set these at the beginning of the report process. Post a large example in the classroom and in the computer lab (if available) to avoid any confusion.

REPORT TITLE

STUDENT'S NAME

DUE DATE

TEACHER'S NAME

CITING ELECTRONIC SOURCES

Whether they are researching for projects or reports, your students need to cite all the resources in which they find usable information. There are printed guidelines for citing books and periodicals, but they must also cite electronic sources such as CD-ROM encyclopedias or reference materials and online sources of information. The following are some basic structures of those bibliography entries.

CD-ROM databases:

Author. "Title of Article." Title of Work. Type of Medium, version. Place of Publication: Publisher, date.

Electronic mail (e-mail):

Sender of e-mail message (e-mail address). "Subject of e-mail." Recipient (recipient's e-mail address). Date of message.

Internet sources (World Wide Web address):

Author. Title of item (or Web page). [Online] Available http://address/filename, date of download or document creation, if available.

Online interview or presentation by speaker:

Name of online speaker. [Online] Available software type: site address, date of session.

Online images, video clips, sound files:

Description of file. [Online Image (or Video Clip or Sound)] Available http://address/filename, date of download or document creation if available.

Web Links:

Classroom Connect: How to Cite Internet Resources
http://www.classroom.net/classroom/CitingNetResources.html

Electronic Sources: MLA Style of Citation
http://www.uvm.edu/~ncrane/estyles/mla.html

Electronic Sources: APA Style of Citation
http://www.uvm.edu/~ncrane/estyles/apa.html

Pitsco's Launch to Citing WWW Addresses
http://www.pitsco.inter.net/p/cite.html

TELECOLLABORATING

Telecollaborating offers you the opportunity to share a classroom activity with teachers and students all around the world. There are projects as simple as sharing experiment data via e-mail to those as in-depth as creating Web sites to compile data sent in from several classrooms. You can either participate in an activity already in place or start one of your own.

NickNacks: Exchanging Information on the Internet offers basic guidelines for creating and maintaining a successful telecollaborating project. They explain many details about transferring data and graphics files. There are suggestions given for creating and sending projects to share with other classes, such as *HyperStudio* and *PageMaker* projects. These two programs also have free viewers available so that other classes can view the final results of your projects. There are also featured projects listed which you and your students can join. One such project was called "Science Now—A Day in the Life of an Ice Cube" in which students collected data from around the world in order to test the hypothesis that global location and climate affect the time it takes an ice cube to totally melt. Classes of all ages were invited to participate and registered with the coordinating teacher and sent their data to the students who analyzed the results and then reported back to all participating classes. NickNacks can be reached at the following address:

> http://www1.minn.net:80/~schubert/exchange.html

OnlineClass sponsors projects such as the Blue Ice Food Webs Unit in which students research the interrelationship between Antartica's environment, physical features, and the wildlife and Rivers of Life: Mississippi Adventure in which students learn about land use, ecology, and watersheds through virtual trips down the Mississippi River or collecting actual data if they live along the river. OnlineClass can be reached at the following address:

> http://www.onlineclass.com.

The Canadian Nature Federation has sponsored a Lady Beetle Survey in which students identify and count lady beetles and report them to a central survey coordinator. The Web site has all the information available for identifying and reporting your survey data. You may want to read what they have and then tailor this activity for researching an insect that appears in your geographic region. You can access this activity at the following address:

> http://www.schoolnet.ca/vp/ladybeetle/ladybuge/index.htm

The KIDLINK organization coordinates projects with students ages 10–15 across the globe. There is information about collaborative projects as well as a place for teachers and parents to gather and talk with each other. Each year KIDLINK posts current projects and archives past projects at the KIDPROJECT site. You may find both these sites online at the following addresses.

> http://www.kidlink.organd
> http://www.kidlink.org/KIDPROJ/

SUPER SUGGESTIONS

If there are ever times when you start to teach a new unit and you have no idea where to begin looking for fresh ideas, then perhaps you should use your Internet resources and look for help from the many teachers all over the world.

E-mail list servers are a great source of ideas, and you may just find that you are a teacher with answers for someone else, too. List servers work through an e-mail server, and the letters sent in to the server are then forwarded to all the other members of the list. You are able to send messages into the server, or you can just receive messages and sift through the ideas. But, the old adage is true: "You get out of something what you put into it." So, contribute, too.

Here are several list servers which serve the technology education community.

e-mail to listproc@ready.cpb.org
In the body of the e-mail, write   subscribe wwwedu Your Name

e-mail to listserv@man.torun.pl
In the body of the e-mail, write   sub APPL-L Your Name

e-mail to listserv@msu.edu
In the body of the e-mail, write   subscribe EDTECH Your Name

These are lists of other list servers which may suit your needs. Be careful to subscribe correctly. In most cases, the subscription e-mail is handled automatically.

Education Links—List Servers
http://www.jrsummit.org/links/edulists.html

List servers—Gopher Listing
gopher://ericir.syr.edu:70/11/Listservs

Educational List Servers
http://mustang.coled.umn.edu/exploration/resource/listserv.html

These are online sites where you may find additional teacher resouces, as well as places to meet other teachers and archives of classroom activities.

Classroom Connect
http://www.classroom.net/

Global SchoolNet Foundation
http://www.gsn.org/

The Landmark Project
http://www.landmark-project.com/home.html

SUPER SUGGESTIONS *(cont.)*

Here are some short suggestions to give you "starters" on other ways to integrate technology into your science curriculum. They were sent in by terrific teachers who wanted to share their ideas.

5th Graders Study the Ocean in Iowa

Although landlocked at Irving Elementary School in Iowa, some students are led through a study of the oceans of the world through the use of the CD-ROM *Oceans Below*, which explores the concepts of scuba gear, ocean exploration, and skin diving. They use *ECO-Adventures in the Ocean* to search for a creature, take its picture, and return to the ship. They also use it to study weather in the ocean, ocean floor exploration, and scuba diving. The program *Field Trip to the Sea* by Sunburst is used to complete a scavenger hunt for sea-dwelling creatures in the database of ocean information. (Another option would be to include *The Great Ocean Rescue* by Tom Snyder Productions.)

8th Graders at The Carol Morgan School of Santo Domingo Scientifically Record Their Lab Data

During physical science classes at The Carol Morgan School, students analyzed their tap water for chloride concentrations. They followed the method from the National Standards book for EPA titration and then used *Microsoft Excel* to program a column in the spreadsheet with a formula to determine the ion concentration. (This could be done with any spreadsheet program, such as *Microsoft Works*, *ClarisWorks*, or *AppleWorks* as long as you instruct the students as to how to input the formula for the calculation. Students enjoy producing professional work, and using the spreadsheet teaches them to utilize the software to perform calculations with a purpose.)

Teacher Uses TV Monitor to Instruct with Lessons from the Computer

A teacher in Suffolk, VA, uses a computer-to-television connector to allow all the students in her class to see what is being done on the computer. From research in a CD-ROM encyclopedia to accessing Internet resources, she is also able to monitor what her students are doing when they are using the computer for independent work. These connections are available for both Mac and PC format computers.

These are examples of ideas you will get if you subscribe to a list server and simply post a request for some help with lesson development. Most teachers are willing to share strategies in an effort to benefit the students. The computer technology facilitates this sharing process.

FINDING LESSON PLANS ONLINE

In addition to sharing lessons with other teachers from list servers or online bulletin board services, you can also find ready-to-go lesson plans online in a variety of locations. The following are a few which you should visit from time to time.

Access Excellence—Genentech
http://www.gene.com/ae/

Access Excellence is a national education program providing biology teachers with access to colleagues, scientists, and current information via the Internet.

Busy Teachers' Web Site
http://www.ceismc.gatech.edu/BusyT/

This is an index of Web links for assorted subject areas. Each subject area has links for lesson plans and classroom activities.

Eastern Connecticut State University
Lesson Plans Using Software
http://www.ecsu.ctstateu.edu/depts/edu/lessons.html

Plans for assorted subject areas, these are all lessons which incorporate some piece of software from simple database and spreadsheet programs to more specific subject area programs and research software.

EUREKA
http://www.cybershopping.com/eureka/

Science lesson plans and resources such as science fair project ideas, educational gift ideas, science catalogs, and science publications can be found at this site.

Florida Geographic Alliance
http://www.firn.edu/~fga/

The Alliance houses teacher resources and is providing as much information as possible through the Web page. This includes many lesson plans by area educators.

Teachers Helping Teachers
http://www.pacificnet.net/~mandel/

This site is for teachers and by teachers. Read the lesson plans contributed by your colleagues and submit some of your own.